Turn Stress into Bliss

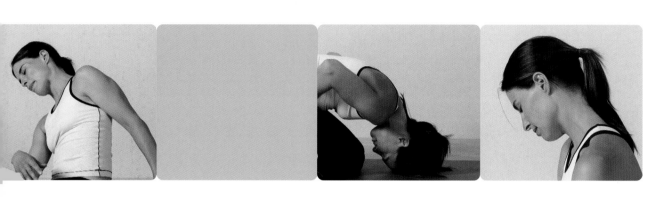

Turn Stress into Bliss

The Proven 8-Week Program for
Better Health, Relaxation, and Stress-Relief

MICHAEL LEE

The founder and director of
Phoenix Rising Yoga Therapy

FAIR WINDS
PRESS
GLOUCESTER, MASSACHUSETTS

DEDICATION

*I dedicate this book to my friends and neighbors of the Katahdin Region
of Maine, where I wrote this book during the summer and fall of 2004.
My view of Katahdin ("greatest mountain") across the beautiful South
Twin Lake, along with the warmth and strength of spirit of those I met
in the area, provided the inspirational backdrop for this book and helped
me find the words I needed and to enjoy every moment of writing.*

Text © 2005 by Michael Lee

First published in the USA in 2005 by
Fair Winds Press
33 Commercial Street
Gloucester, MA 01930

08 07 06 05 04   1 2 3 4 5

ISBN 1-59233-117-3

Library of Congress Cataloging-in-Publication Data available

Cover design by Yee Design
Book design by Yee Design

Printed and bound in Singapore

The information in this book is for educational purposes only. It is not intended
to replace the advice of a physician or medical practitioner. Please see your
health care provider before beginning any new health program.

CONTENTS

How Stress Affects Your Health

BY TIMOTHY MCCALL, MD

FOREWORD

If you think of "stress-related" health problems, an upset stomach, trouble falling asleep, or a tension headache might come to mind. But increasing scientific evidence indicates that stress can be a factor in life-threatening conditions from heart attacks to depression to hip fractures.

When scientists talk about the stress-response system, they are referring to a complex web of events that ramp up the body to deal with an acute crisis. Responding to a perceived physical threat, the body shunts energy away from restorative functions like digestion and reproduction, mediated by the parasympathetic nervous system. The sympathetic nervous system kicks in, which among other things increases blood flow to the large muscles that help you defend yourself or run away. This is the so-called "fight or flight" system.

Stress hormones such as adrenaline and cortisol are also released. In response, blood pressure and heart rate go up and breathing quickens. Blood sugar and other energy stores are mobilized as fuel for whatever challenge you are about to face. In case you are injured, your blood begins to clot more easily.

This built-in stress-response system is well-adapted to acute crises but can lead to all kinds of problems if it doesn't gets switched off. Blood clots increase the risk of a heart attack or a stroke, as does high blood pressure. Elevated levels of cortisol are associated with everything from depression to osteoporosis to overeating and weight gain. And while the immune system initially gets stronger during an acutely stressful event, it starts functioning less well if the situation goes on too long, raising the risk of serious infections and autoimmune diseases.

The ancient human stress-response system isn't well adapted to non-physical modern world stressors such as work deadlines, disagreements with family members, or even abstract ideas about whether you are happy or fulfilled. If you repeatedly mull over these problems, the chemical and physical changes that were designed to deal with an acute threat to physical health—and then shut off—remain activated. Such mental tape loops can thus turn abstract worries into concrete threats to health, and even to life itself.

Beyond the harmful effects on the body, being stuck in a mind-generated tape loop is unpleasant. It can make you feel terrible, preoccupied, and full of dread. This is where yoga can prove so helpful.

Yoga offers a series of tools including postures, meditation, and breathing exercises which induce deep relaxation and can, sometimes within minutes, slow down an overactive stress-response system. One of the great insights of the ancient yoga masters is that when you move and breathe with awareness, it calms the nervous system and slows down the tape loops in the mind. When the inner monologue slows, most people experience a sense of peace, relaxation, and a feeling of being centered.

At first, this only happens when you are doing yoga and perhaps for a short time afterwards. But if you maintain a steady practice, you become more aware and can tap into the tranquility you find in yoga throughout the rest of your day.

This sense of inner calm can make you feel more grateful for what you have, appreciate the beauty around you (which you might not have noticed), and help you realize that some of the stuff you're getting bent out of shape about may, ultimately, not be very important. And that may be the best stress-reduction method of all.

In *Turn Stress into Bliss*, Michael Lee illuminates, in a heartfelt and accessible manner, the Phoenix Rising approach to stress-reduction and personal transformation. Follow his eight-week plan and you may discover that you are, as Joseph Campbell used to say, following your bliss.

Timothy McCall, M.D., is the Medical Editor of Yoga Journal and the author of Yoga as Medicine. He can be found on the Web at www.DrMcCall.com

Introduction

WHAT IS STRESS? WHAT IS BLISS?

Let's deal with the second question first. I have a friend who is a chiropractor, and he sees a lot of people with chronic back pain. When he first meets a patient, he likes to find out more about the individual so he can determine the best course of treatment. He asks several questions, including, "How long has it been since you had some real fun?" He says he hears three basic responses. First: "Oh, just last week I took my kids to an amusement park, and we had a blast." This type of patient will be easy to treat, and the problem is most likely just a temporary physical dysfunction. Second: "Well, doc, it's been a while since I had any real fun." This patient might have other things going on in his life that could be contributing to his physical problem. Treatment won't be as easy and may take longer. The third response is the most interesting: "Fun? What is that? Could you define that for me?" My friend has a real problem on his hands with this type of patient. She is probably not very well connected to herself physically or emotionally and prefers to have her life defined by an external authority rather than by her own genuine, unique experiences.

If you think about it, fun is different for different people. But anyone who has ever had fun knows what it is. The same could be said of bliss. I recently had one of those magical, unforgettable days. When I write, I like to come to my simple lakefront "camp" in the North Woods of Maine. I have a spectacular view of Katahdin, the highest mountain in Maine, with a lake in the foreground. On this morning, the air was still, and the lake was the calmest I had ever seen it. The water shimmered like glass. I was so awestruck by the beauty in front of my eyes that instead of doing the next thing, I paused and sat down and took it all in for the next 10 minutes. Later in the day, the sunset was even more beautiful. The scenery, my feelings, and my connection to life all seemed to come together in one instant to create an overall magnificent experience—a sensual and spiritual orgasm without sex. On both occasions, I was in *bliss*, at least according to my definition of it, and no one else's definition could have affected my experience of it. It simply was what it was.

BLISS CAN ONLY BE PRESENT WHEN STRESS IS ABSENT— OR AT LEAST HANDLED

Now, I believe that my capacity to experience bliss has a lot to do with what is happening overall in my life. To use my experience at the lake as an example, if my life had recently been stressful, would I have been able to notice the lake and the view right in front of me, or would my mind have been so busy with worries and my to-do list that I would not have taken the time to notice it? Or if I had noticed, would I have ignored it in order to accomplish the next "important" thing?

The amount of stress many of us have in our lives makes us unable to experience as much bliss as we potentially could. We are so busy getting things done and trying to accomplish more and more that we lose the opportunity for bliss—those peaceful moments that enrich and soothe us.

When life places us in unknown and uncomfortable situations for long enough, we become like fish out of water. In response, we flap vigorously to try to regain our comfort level, but trying to swim on land just doesn't work. Something is missing: the water. We think we can survive if we just swim harder and faster, but the result is the same. There is no progress, and we don't get back to where we want to be.

Whenever we create situations in our lives that defy our deep inner wisdom and we continue to do things that are not in our best long-term interest, we begin to remove ourselves from the "water." This can happen in very subtle and barely noticeable ways. It can also happen when we try to do more than we can handle at any given time. I recall reading a stress checklist that listed many life-changing events that we all experience from time to time. Each event had a score so I could calculate my total stress level. If I had two or more life-changing events happening at the same time, I had a good chance of being seriously under stress. For example, a new relationship accompanied by a change in residence; the death of a loved one accompanied by a change in career or the arrival of a newborn; or any similar combination would most likely be enough to put most of us over the edge with stress.

Why does change produce stress? Because change requires us to adapt—to do things differently from the way we have grown accustomed to doing them—and doing things differently is not always easy. It can put us on edge. Remember the dinosaurs and why they disappeared? The climate changes they had to face were too stressful, so they died. They simply could not adapt. Are we in danger as those dinosaurs were?

Think about life in our 21st century for a moment. Change is all around us. Technology during the last 10 years alone has produced more changes to the way we do things than did the entire century before that. We've also changed socially. No longer does the traditional family consist of one income earner and one homemaker. Usually both parents work—that is, if the family has two parents. Many families today have just one parent. The demands of family are greater and more complicated than they were in the past. We have less time to relax. And when we do find time, the demands of air travel in our new security-conscious world make getting to and from a vacation with a family in tow anything but relaxing.

Potential sources of stress are all around us in just about every aspect of our lives, so it's not surprising that stress-related disorders top the list of reasons for visits to doctors or that all kinds of new stress-related disorders are appearing. A recent study cosponsored by the Mailman School of Public Health at Columbia University finds that women who worry a lot may also suffer from ulcers. Researchers think that out-of-control stress may activate a bacterium known as *H. pylori*, setting off a chain reaction inside the body that causes ulcers to develop. Evidence also suggests that stress causes fluctuations in sex hormones in women, which may lead to more-severe body and mood changes during menstruation, pregnancy, and perimenopause.

The good news is that stress is not something that just happens to us; it's something over which we have control. There are two important ways we can tackle it. First, we can look at our lifestyles and see what triggers stress. This sounds simple, but it really is not, because we are often unaware that we are under stress or unsure of what causes the stress in our lives. Furthermore, we are often unwilling to change our ways even if we are aware of our stressors. Like the dinosaurs, we have a high propensity to just keep on doing the same old things in our lives day after day. Of course, we rationalize our choices with statements such as, "Oh, I really should be taking on less, but that's hard to do with young children. They need so much. Maybe when they are older, I'll be able to slow down."

The second stress-control solution is the one I like the best: We need to build up some "inner muscle" so we can handle the stress in our lives more easily. In the same way we work out and lift weights so that over time we can increase the amount of weight our bodies can handle, we can work on how we respond to stress to increase our capacity to handle it. Stressful situations don't necessarily make us stressed. What causes our stress is how we respond to such situations. Put two people in the same stressful situation, and you might be surprised to find that one goes down under the burden while the other comes away laughing. Stress is not the enemy. We are the enemy.

Therefore, if we want to turn our stress into bliss, we need to work from the inside and develop a capacity to handle stress. These skills help us develop the capacity to change right along with it. We become very undinosaur-like in our approach to life and actually enjoy making the changes that lead to more bliss, more fun, more connection, and more growth and learning.

So think of the things you'll be asked to do in the 8-week program outlined in this book as inner exercise. Just like any exercise, doing it daily makes a huge difference. The most difficult part of this whole program is simply making that commitment. Are you ready?

ABOUT THE PROGRAM

This book is based on work I and my staff at Phoenix Rising Yoga Therapy conducted with groups of people who had stress-related physical symptoms. One group of 10 was composed of people diagnosed with irritable bowel syndrome (IBS). We gave each group member a questionnaire at the beginning of the session to explain their symptoms and the extent to which their lives were affected by them. At our first meeting, we acknowledged that group members shared a common disorder and many of the same symptoms, and then we did not mention the disease again for the following 8 weeks. We also did not treat the disorder directly. Instead, we did the exercises that are in this book each week, just as you will be asked to do. At the end of 8 weeks, we gave the participants the same survey. They reported an overall 55 percent reduction in their symptoms of IBS even though they hadn't paid any direct attention to them. How could this be, you may ask? The answer is both simple and complex. By doing the exercises daily for 8 weeks, they were able to build the inner muscle that copes with potentially stressful situations. The potential stress in their lives lost the power to produce the symptoms in their bodies. Many of them also made some significant changes to their lives during the 8 weeks and eliminated many of the sources of their stress. As a result of both of these changes, they experienced less pain and less "disease."

I want to issue a word of caution. As we don't know whether symptoms are stress related or not without a thorough diagnosis, I am not suggesting you throw away your prescriptions or stop seeing your doctor if you are someone under treatment for a disorder that you may suspect is stress related. Instead, try this program for 8 weeks along with whatever other treatment you are receiving, and see what happens. Then have a conversation with your doctor if you think you have found a way to better help you deal with your problem.

CHAPTER 1

How to Use This Program to Create Real Change

FOR 8 CONSECUTIVE WEEKS, YOU WILL BE ASKED TO DEVOTE 40 minutes of each day to a set of exercises and tasks. Every week will have a focus. On at least 6 days of each week, you will practice a short yoga routine or spend some time sitting in silent meditation.

You will also spend time integrating what you notice about yourself and your daily life. This integration is very important; it's what distinguishes this program from other kinds of yoga and meditation programs. To effectively turn the stress in your life into bliss, you need to become more aware of what is happening in your life and what needs to change in your day-to-day routine.

In addition, you will have some other exercises or tasks to do each week to encourage further awareness and to support you in the changes you want to make. These exercises will help bring greater clarity and direction to your life; they will complement the benefits you derive from your daily yoga and meditation practice. This program will help you begin to live more mindfully and healthfully by requiring you to spend time on yourself, with yourself, and noticing yourself. As a first step toward looking inward, take the Simple Bliss Test in Appendix Two of this book. This test will give you an idea of the extent of the stress and bliss in your life right now. Then, at the end of the program, you can take the test again and see how far you have come toward your goal of turning your stress into bliss.

YOU WILL CREATE YOUR BLISS

This program is based on two powerful principles: first, that regular yoga practice can increase happiness and decrease stress, and second, that each one of us is unique in how we create our own stress and our own bliss. When you have greater happiness and less stress in your life, abundant health is much easier to come by. Conversely, a stressful life without joy can lead to disease and premature death. To change from stress to bliss requires commitment, but it also requires courage. How important is it to you to change your life? If it's important, then it's worth making the commitment to put aside the time for this program. But you have to decide that.

One suggestion I have to help you keep your commitment is to take it one day at a time. As you look at your calendar for tomorrow, decide when to schedule your 40 minutes and make it a priority in your day—above anything else you do. This will be tough. There are all kinds of good reasons we come up with for putting other things in front of ourselves. Don't compromise. Each day, schedule your 40-minute commitment for the following day. You can give yourself a day off after you've completed 6 days in 1 week, but if you want to practice on all 7 days to keep a routine going, that's fine, too.

I also recommend that you enlist the support of your friends and family. Let them know what you are doing and why you are doing it, and ask for their encouragement. Ultimately, though, your success will be dependent on your own willingness to make this program a priority for 8 weeks and to make changes in your life that reduce stress and let you experience more joy.

WHERE WILL YOU FIND 40 MINUTES?

Now that you are ready to commit 40 minutes of the day to this program, you are probably wondering which 40. My response is always, "Whenever it works best for you." I wrote most of this book you are reading in the early hours of the morning—between 5:00 and 7:00. Why? That's my best time to write. I have few distractions, I feel fresh in my mind, and my writing just seems to flow at that time of the day. Likewise, I practice my daily yoga and meditation routines in the morning, too—sometimes before I write and sometimes after, but always before 8:00. In my life with children, spouse, job, chores, and other responsibilities, the day seems to get very busy after 8:00. My mind also gets busy and can easily rationalize that I have more-urgent tasks to do other than yoga or meditation. So if I'm going to take time for myself, it has to be early in the day or late in the day, when most everyone else is in bed. I'm not a night owl, and evening doesn't suit me. I often find that by then I'm tired and just want to relax or go to bed. So I choose early morning as my time.

Evening might work for you, though. You have to decide when in your day you can find 40 minutes for yourself without interruption. You may find it helpful to get into a routine of doing the program at the same time and place each day, but that's not essential for success. What is essential is that you do find that 40 minutes every day and that you do it by marking it on your calendar the day before and planning accordingly. For me, because early morning is my time, my planning includes going to bed at a reasonably early hour. I set a bedtime that will give my next day's 40 minutes a 100 percent chance of happening.

As you begin to notice the positive changes that come to you from this program, the temptation to drop it and go back to old ways could be very strong. This is because change doesn't happen in single doses. One change invites more changes and in many areas of life. And the prospect of too much change can be overwhelming. For example, Janet, a 48-year-old woman who did this program, realized that as she became less stressed and started feeling better about herself, she also noticed how much of herself she was giving in certain relationships. Before, her codependent friends made her feel good when she always gave to them. Once she felt better about herself, she began to notice that she no longer needed those relationships in the same way. But to give them up and find new friends would have demanded incredible courage. The familiar path was easier, even if it was less fulfilling. She stopped doing her 8-week program and went back to her old ways—but only for a while. She returned to the program 6 months later. This time, she made the changes that were being called for in her life from her increased awareness.

Some of the things you will be doing along with your yoga and meditation practice are drinking and eating mindfully, walking, performing self-care exercises, organizing your life and living space, journaling, and learning more about yourself. Each week will have a focus or a theme, and each day of that week will contain exercises that relate to that focus. As mentioned previously, the program requires a 6-day-per-week commitment of 40 minutes per day. That is just 4 hours per week of your time. There are 168 hours in every week, and all you have to do is commit to spending 4 of them focused on yourself.

This program will give you directions on what to do during those six 40-minute time slots and also how to do the various exercises. The *how* is just as important (maybe even more so) than the what. You will be asked to do things mindfully. This means really noticing what happens moment to moment as you do everything. You will soon see this practice carry over into the rest of your daily activities. When you are clear about the choices you are making, then you can adapt and make different choices. Many of us go about our days in a kind of foglike dream, with life just happening to us as we go. We live in more of a state of reaction than a state of choice. When we notice how much of this is occurring in our lives, we can begin to change it.

The yoga and meditation practices provide the training ground for this noticing. It's very important that you follow the "how" directions in these practices. Anyone can do a series of yoga postures and not notice anything much along the way. It takes a lot more focus to notice moment to moment what is happening in your body and mind as you engage in a posture, hold it, breathe fully and deeply, feel it, then slowly release from the posture and pause before transitioning to the next. This constitutes a mindful yoga practice. The same is true with meditation. You could sit and meditate for a given period and just be dragged by your mind from one train of thought to another. Here, in the 10 or 20 minutes at a time that you sit and meditate, you will be asked to notice your thoughts, label them, accept them, and watch for what happens next.

CHAPTER 2

Tools You Will Need

THIS BOOK IS YOUR PRIMARY TOOL TO GUIDE YOU THROUGH your 8-week program, so you might want to read it in its entirety before you begin—say, in the week prior. It will be easier to follow the directions in this book if you read them a couple of times first and then do the exercises or practices.

Alternatively, you could use a voice recorder to tape yourself speaking the directions slowly and then listen to the directions as you do the exercises. Prerecorded audio materials that you can use are listed in Appendix One of this book. Although you can do the program without them, you may find it easier to listen to the directions on a CD rather than reading them several times before you start.

There are a few other tools and props you will need:

- **A timer to let you know when a set time period has passed.** This will enable you to focus on the exercise without needing to interrupt yourself to look at a watch or clock. If you have a watch with an alarm that's easy to set, this can serve as a timer.

- **A place in your house where you can do your daily practice.** Find somewhere that will be free from interruptions and noise. Prepare your place by cleaning and tidying. You should have enough room to lie on the floor and stretch your arms and legs in all four directions without touching anything.

- **Two mats for your yoga practice.** One should be the typical "sticky mat"; the other, a clean and firm heavy blanket.

- **A firm pillow or cushion about 4 to 6 inches high.** It should be firm enough to support your buttocks at least 3 to 4 inches off the floor.

- **A straight-back chair in which to sit comfortably for meditation.** It should support your back and be the right height to allow your feet to remain firmly planted on the floor.

- **A journal.** If you don't own one, go out and purchase one. It's simply a book of blank pages in which you can write. It is private and should not be left around for anyone else to read. It will be a place where you can record from time to time what you are noticing and learning about yourself and what you are wanting in life. Recording such self-reflections is a very important part of this program. Along with your journal, you will need a pen or pencil to write with.

The above items are the essentials. You can add some optional extras if you want. Some people like to have a candle in their place. By performing the small ritual of lighting the candle at the beginning of your daily practice and extinguishing it at the end, you will mark the time that you are setting aside for your program. Taking a few extra moments to do this can make a difference in your mind-set as you transition into and out of this special time each day.

If you choose to record in your own voice some of the written directions for the various exercises and practices in this book, you will need a voice recorder/player.

You may also want to include in your place a special object or picture that reminds you of yourself in a state of feeling great about life. I have a picture of myself and two of my older children white-water rafting. The exhilaration I felt at the time that picture was taken was one of my peak moments in life. I use it to remind myself that life is good.

If there are other things that will help you feel more at home and comfortable being with yourself, then go ahead and have them in your place. Just make sure to keep the area relatively simple and free of clutter or anything that might distract you unnecessarily.

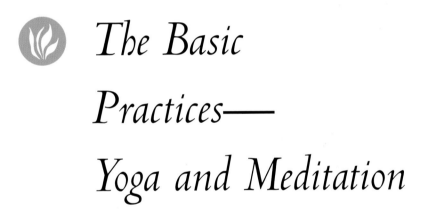

CHAPTER 3

The Basic Practices— Yoga and Meditation

YOGA

Although yoga is now very popular in the Western world and is obviously an accepted practice in many circles, it has sometimes been seen as mysterious and almost as a pseudoreligion. Some practitioners of yoga tend to get off on its esoteric aspects and cultlike trappings. This is unfortunate, as it tends to give yoga a bad rap and perhaps prevents more people from trying it. Along with this, yoga is often popularly characterized by its extreme physical aspects. I'm sure you've heard statements like, "Oh, I can't do yoga. My body won't bend like a pretzel!" People tend to think that in order to practice yoga, they need to look like the model on the front cover of *Yoga Journal*. The truth is, yoga is practiced my millions of people in the world, and very few of them look like that model or ever will. I hope that if you follow the practices outlined in this book, you will appreciate that yoga is indeed for every *body*.

The yoga part of your practice will consist of a selection of yoga postures and exercises chosen from the "Complete Posture List" in Appendix Three. You won't have to think about which ones to choose. We have selected a set of postures from the sequence for each week of the 8 in the program. You will be practicing much the same set of postures in any given week with some additions and variations as we go. The weeks are sequenced to give you an easy introduction to yoga if you have never practiced before and also to provide you with guidance in using the Phoenix Rising approach.

Remember, different schools of yoga and different teachers emphasize different aspects of this old practice. This doesn't mean one way is right and another wrong. Your chosen method should depend on what your purpose is. The Phoenix Rising approach outlined in this book is great for beginners, but it's great for more-experienced yoga practitioners, as well. It will be a valuable experience for anyone who may have focused only on the physical aspects of yoga without exploring the deeper aspects from the inside. This approach is designed to give you the maximum gain in self-awareness and to help you get to know yourself at a very deep level. For that reason, it may not seem as physically demanding as some other "brands" of yoga.

What might be difficult, however, is the focus that you are asked to apply. Unlike approaches to yoga that concentrate on the physical form, the Phoenix Rising approach in large part focuses on what is happening moment to moment in your total experience. So even if you are someone who has been doing yoga for years, I invite you to once again become a beginner as you start this program. Try it out. Don't worry if it's not hard enough for you physically. Later on you'll be able to apply the Phoenix Rising principles to whatever kind of physical yoga you choose. For now, though, I want to offer you a time to use yoga as a tool for self-knowledge and self-awareness. To do that, we need to start with a physical practice that is so simple that it doesn't distract you from the deeper purpose, but supports that purpose from a mind-body perspective.

Although the program is appropriate for beginners, some preparation is useful before you begin the 8-week session. If you live in an area where there is a Phoenix Rising yoga teacher or yoga therapy practitioner, you could take a one-on-one session and be guided through the practice once or twice before you begin. You can also take a little time before beginning the program to follow the directions for the sequence for Week One in the book. This may take you an hour or more, which you could break up into a few shorter time slots. What is important is at least getting to know the physical mechanics of the postures. There is no time built into the 8-week schedule for you to learn them. The 8-week program is meant to be experiential. That means you are experiencing yoga, not learning how to do it. So you will need to decide for yourself how to best prepare to begin the program. The sequence is also available on CD from Phoenix Rising (see Appendix One), and following it a few times could be an excellent way to prepare for the program.

For those who want more yoga than what is outlined in the week-by-week guide for this program, you have some other options available. Be warned, however, that it is very easy to take the attitude that creates stress in your life and transfer it to your yoga practice. If you tend to be an overachiever in life, I would suggest you approach your yoga in a different manner. Try just sticking to the basics of this program and resist the urge to want to do advanced or difficult or demanding postures. The basics in this program have been proven to work for people dealing with stress-related symptoms. At the same time, I realize that many folks reading this book may have practiced yoga for some time already, and they may be ready for postures that yoga newcomers are not. If this describes you, then you may want to supplement with your own postures or those from the list in Appendix Four. The program will work for you as long as you can apply the Phoenix Rising approach to any yoga posture you are practicing. To learn this approach, I suggest you follow at least the routine for Week One before substituting more-difficult postures.

This program requires you to practice for only 40 minutes per day on at least 6 days a week. If you happen to have more time available, then you can add postures to your practice. Later in the program, you will learn about a longer yoga sequence that you can follow when time permits.

The detail in the following chapters covers two main aspects of your yoga practice. It gives you physical guidance: how to move your body into each posture or exercise, how to breathe, how to maintain proper alignment, how to prevent injury, and how to "play the edge" in each posture (an essential part of the

Phoenix Rising approach). It also provides you with the guidance needed for your inner work: how to focus your awareness and what questions to ask yourself, how to observe and witness yourself, how to handle distractions, how to be with yourself as your inner journey begins to unfold, and what to do with what you discover. Both of these aspects are essential to the Phoenix Rising approach to yoga. In order to accommodate both, the physical descriptions are not necessarily as precise as those you might see in other yoga books. However, you should find them easy to follow and adequate to cover the basics of entering and releasing from the postures. You will sometimes find suggested variations that should allow the sequences to be adapted for anybody. If you have any difficulty with the postures, check out the resources in Appendix One of this book, and you'll be sure to find a way to overcome it.

You'll also notice that English common names are used for the postures rather than the Sanskrit names used in some yoga classes. While Sanskrit is a beautiful language that adds color and meaning to yoga for many, I do not consider it essential in order to gain benefits from a yoga practice. After you have been practicing for a while and have begun to derive both the physical and inner benefits of yoga, you may choose to explore some of the more esoteric aspects of yoga, including Sanskrit terminology. For now, though, this could distract from the essence of the practices we want to focus upon. Remember, the main purpose of this program is to help you turn stress in your life into bliss. To fulfill this purpose, I have chosen to emphasize only those elements of the broad field of yoga that my Phoenix Rising colleagues and I have found will do that.

MEDITATION

In addition to doing yoga postures and using your body as a way of connecting to yourself at a deeper level, you will practice meditation as another way of connecting. The Phoenix Rising approach to meditation is perhaps similar to other forms of meditation you might be familiar with, such as mindfulness, or *vipassana*, meditation. But some features of the approach also make it a little different. Many people have difficulty with meditation for various reasons, so this program tries to keep the practice simple. It also tries to be value neutral: It should work for anybody, regardless of his or her spiritual belief, interest in spirituality, or particular approach to life. Although many of the existing meditation practices that come from various traditions might share this intention, the directions they offer often suggest some particular ideal state of being you need to achieve. My hope is that you won't find that with the Phoenix Rising method of meditation that is outlined for you in this book.

CHAPTER 4

 The First 4 Weeks—Themes, Yoga Practice, Meditation Practice, Journaling, Other Exercises

WEEK ONE

Here is your first week's schedule, which begins on Sunday. The theme for this first week is befriending your body.

Your body is a key player in your success with this program. It is through your body that you will learn the most and through your body that you will change everything in your life that needs to change. So, just like a carpenter who goes to the hardware store and buys a new tool, early on in this program you will need to learn how to use the tool you call your body. The first question you might ask yourself is, "What kind of a relationship do I have with my body?" And before you answer, it might be good to visit with your body for a while to find out what it has to say. There will be lots of opportunity in your practice in this first week to spend time visiting with your body and seeing what it might be like to make friends with it.

SUNDAY

Self-Presence Exercise and Intention Setting: **5 minutes**

Yoga Practice Sequence: **20 minutes**

Meditation and Integration: **10 minutes**

Journaling: **5 minutes**

* *Drink 8 glasses of water today*
* *Perform 1 small act today to support your intention*
* *Schedule a bubble bath for Wednesday*

MONDAY

Self-Presence Exercise and Intention Setting: **5 minutes**

Body Scan Meditation Exercise: **15 minutes**

Walking: **10 minutes**

Integration: **5 minutes**

Journaling: **5 minutes**

* *Drink 8 glasses of water today*
* *Perform 1 small act today to support your intention*

TUESDAY

Self-Presence Exercise and Intention Setting: **5 minutes**

Yoga Practice Sequence: **20 minutes**

Meditation and Integration: **10 minutes**

Journaling: **5 minutes**

* *Drink 8 glasses of water today*
* *Perform 1 small act today to support your intention*
* *Buy a bubble-bath packet for tomorrow*

WEDNESDAY

Self-Presence Exercise and Intention Setting: **5 minutes**

Body Scan Meditation Exercise: **15 minutes**

Integration: **5 minutes**

Journaling: **5 minutes**

Bubble Bath: **10 minutes**

* *Drink 8 glasses of water today*
* *Perform 1 small act today to support your intention*

Week One

Set aside 40-45 minutes each day to practice.

THURSDAY

Self-Presence Exercise and Intention Setting: **5 minutes**

Yoga Practice Sequence: **20 minutes**

Meditation and Integration: **10 minutes**

Journaling: **5 minutes**

* *Drink 8 glasses of water today*
* *Perform 1 small act today to support your intention*

FRIDAY

Self-Presence Exercise and Intention Setting: **5 minutes**

Body Scan Meditation Exercise: **15 minutes**

Walking: **10 minutes**

Integration: **5 minutes**

Journaling: **5 minutes**

* *Drink 8 glasses of water today*
* *Perform 1 small act today to support your intention*

SATURDAY

(If you have already completed 6 days this week, then this day is optional. If you don't want to practice, spend an hour doing something you really love to do.)

Self-Presence Exercise and Intention Setting: **5 minutes**

Yoga Practice Sequence: **20 minutes**

Meditation and Integration: **10 minutes**

Journaling: **5 minutes**

* *Drink 8 glasses of water today*
* *Perform 1 small act today to support your intention*

Self-Presence Exercise

Sit in a comfortable chair that's not too soft. You need to be able to sit with your feet on the floor and your back long and straight but not strained. Place your hands in your lap with your palms facing up and the backs of your hands resting on your thighs. Set your timer for 3 minutes and close your eyes. Begin to notice your breath entering and leaving your body. Don't make any effort to change your breathing; just notice it. Then notice your body as it receives your breath. Notice your feet on the floor, your legs, your hips, your buttocks, your abdomen, your chest and shoulders, your arms, your neck, and your head. Then notice what it's like for you to focus on your body in this way. Feel it fully: Notice what it's like to be right here right now living in this body. In particular, watch for any thoughts that might creep into your awareness. Remember that there is nothing else you need to be doing. Just keep your eyes closed, breathe, and simply be present, or attentive, to your body in the moment. Continue to observe how this feels for 3 minutes.

After 3 minutes, open your eyes but stay sitting in the chair. Ask yourself what happened during those 3 minutes. What did you notice about your body? In particular, what did you notice about your relationship with your body? Do you have a good relationship, or do you not get along too well? There is no right or wrong answer to these questions. Your answers will give you valuable information about yourself. As you are going to use your body as your teacher in much of this program, it's important to find out what kind of relationship you have with this teacher.

Take Control of Your Relationship with Your Body

So let's say you discover that your relationship with your body is lacking in some way. Maybe you discover you hate your body. Instead of beating yourself up about that, just notice it as your reaction for now. Maybe even say it to yourself: "I just discovered that I hate my body" or whatever statement best describes what you found out. Maybe there is a story associated with what you discovered. Tell the story to yourself. Acknowledge the reasons the relationship got to be that way. Also ask yourself how you would like this relationship to be if you want it to change.

Now here's the kicker: The only person who can change your relationship with your body is you. Your body can't do it for you. It's like the words in that famous speech by John F. Kennedy: "Ask not what your body can do for you; ask what you can do for your body."

If we want to create a better relationship with anyone or anything, we can usually begin with a little acceptance and forgiveness. So whatever has happened between you and your body in the past, can you simply accept that? Take the

advice in the famous Beatles song and "let it be." And if your body has let you down in any way in the past, you can now forgive it. We know that relationships thrive with attention. Children do all kinds of things to get our attention, and so do our bodies. Like children, they tend to act out even more if they get negative attention. If I hate my body because it doesn't give me what I want in life, it might respond even more negatively. But if I can find a way to take care of it...maybe even to love it a little, it just might respond in a different way. So ask, "What could I do this week to show my body that I accept it, forgive it, and love it?"

Ways to Show Love to Your Body

If you can't think of anything, here is a list of possibilities:

- Get a massage.

- Take a hot bath or Jacuzzi.

- Go for a leisurely walk.

- Dance to your favorite music.

- Go swimming.

- Play catch or some other game with children or friends that invites having fun with your body.

Notice that I haven't put things on the list such as go to the gym for a work-out. That kind of activity can be on your list, but only if it meets certain conditions. If you are someone who can go to the gym and work out and really enjoy it and feel good during the session from start to finish, then it qualifies as a befriending-your-body exercise. But if you go to the gym and grunt and strain and push your limits and hate every minute of it, this does not qualify as befriending your body. You know what I mean? If this is the case, you will need to find a different way to make friends with your body.

Intention Setting

After you have completed the self-presence exercise, take a moment to ask yourself, "What is it that I want to create for myself from doing this practice today?" It may help to remember what attracted you to pick up this book. Ask yourself, "What do I want to create in my life and how will doing yoga today help me to fulfill that?" The answer to these questions becomes your intention for your practice today. Do this each time you practice, because you will most likely notice changes. As you make progress and begin to realize your goals, new purposes will emerge.

For me, yoga was originally for myself. I wanted to become more relaxed, more healthy, and more aware. Over the years, my intention has changed many times, although sometimes the changes have been only subtle variations of my original intention. Now most times my intention centers around my family. I want to be the most supportive husband, dad, and guide for my family. I can best serve these roles when I am centered, aware, focused, and relaxed. My yoga practice gives me all of that and more.

Don't worry if your intention seems very simple or not altruistic or noble. Don't worry if it seems self-centered. It's important that you honor where you are in your life and be true to that. So if your intention is something as straight-forward as "I just want to be happy," then accept that for now as your truth.

Yoga Practice Sequence

1. Wake-Up/Warm-Up Exercise

2. Falling-Out Breath/Stillness

3. Neck and Shoulder Stretch

4. Three-Part Breath

5. Swinging Twist

6. Side Bend (Half-Moon)

7. Back Bend

8. Standing Forward Bend

9. Half Facedown Boat

10. Cobra

11. Knees to Chest

12. Corpse

You will be doing the same basic set of yoga poses and exercises, with minor variations, throughout the entire program. You might think this is boring. If so, you are missing the fact that although the physical mechanics of the exercises are the same, your experience will be different every time you do them. But in order to know that, you have to pay attention. As much as you can, pay attention to every little nuance. What are you feeling, thinking, experiencing moment to moment? Each day this week, see if you can notice the "newness" of the same exercise every time you do it.

Wake-Up/Warm-Up Exercise

1 Sit on the floor in Easy Pose—legs crossed, body relaxed, hands on thighs, or any way you feel comfortable. After 10 or so easy breaths, begin to connect with your body. Do this slowly and with one part of the body at a time.

2 Start with your neck and head. Notice your head. Let it begin to make small movements from side to side and forward and back. Slow the movements down as much as you can. As you slowly move your head and neck, pay attention to what you notice—the feel of it.

3 Allow your shoulders to join in on the moving. Roll the shoulders around one way and then the other. Shrug them up toward your ears and let them drop. Focus on deep *falling-out breaths*—that is, let each exhale just fall out as you make a long *haaaah* sound. Enjoy it.

4 Invite your arms and hands to join in the gentle and easy movements. After that, involve your whole upper body. Now you are moving your head, neck, shoulders, arms, hands, and upper body. If possible, let the movements just happen, allowing your body to decide how to move.

5 Begin to engage the lower body. To do this, you might want to roll onto the floor from your sitting position. You can lie facedown or on your back. As you engage your hips, legs, and feet, don't forget to keep including all the upper-body parts. One way I like to approach this exercise is to imagine I'm about 2 years old and discovering my body with conscious awareness for the first time by moving the various parts to see what they do, where they go, and how they feel in different positions. Notice that the way I'm asking you to practice this exercise

continued on next page >

is probably different from what you are used to when you think of body exercise. It's not about "doing it right" or "no pain, no gain." It's really more about play and presence. Just play by engaging your body and being present to it: Be aware of what you are thinking, feeling, and noticing. You don't need to fix or change anything about what you notice.

6 After you have engaged your whole body in movement in a lying-down position, come to a hands-and-knees position and continue the movements there for a minute. Then come to your hands and feet and try them there. Finally, bend your

knees slightly and allow your body to gently unfold to a standing position. Continue the movements for a minute further.

7 Let the movements slow down and eventually stop. Stand in stillness but continue to breathe and "let it be." *Haaaah*. Make sure you notice what is happening now, and think about what you noticed along the way. Overall, was this experience in moving your various body parts an enjoyable one, or did you feel uncomfortable?

❁

Remember, with this Phoenix Rising approach to yoga and meditation, you are not trying to create a particular state of being. I trust that you will ultimately do that for yourself in good time. It's more important now that you validate your experience—regardless of whether it's good, bad, or indifferent. It's not supposed to be a certain way. This is not that kind of yoga. This is the yoga of self-discovery and self-inquiry, and all experiences are valid. Yes, you will be able to turn your stress into bliss but not without first understanding what is in the way of the bliss. This approach requires you to first be aware of "what is" rather than rushing to create "what's desirable." Through recognition and acceptance of "what is," the underlying stress-producing issues in our lives will gradually lose their power over us. Trying to prematurely transcend these issues by creating a false sense of bliss will only give the issues more power over us. So if there is anything you don't like in this opening yoga exercise or in any area of this program, just notice that dislike—and whatever other talk in your mind accompanies it—and continue anyway. Reread the directions tomorrow and do it again. Notice what happens then, and the next day, and the next, and so on.

Falling-Out Breath/Stillness

The first exercise was to help you connect to your body. Notice how you feel at the end as you stand and experience your body in stillness again after having moved it around for a few minutes. Take a deep breath, letting the exhale just fall out. Focus on this falling-out breath for several breaths and notice the stillness that follows each breath after you let it go. You are ready to begin the next part of the sequence.

Neck and Shoulder Stretch

1 Stand or sit to begin. Let your back and spine be long, your breathing deep and easy. Close your eyes. Let your head fall to the left a little. Place your left hand up over the top of your head to rest on your right ear. Take a deep breath in, and as you exhale, allow the weight of your left arm to take your head a little farther to the left so you are feeling a stretch on the right side of your neck. Don't stretch too much or too little. Find your edge, the best stretch possible that is short of any pain. Let your breath just fall out with a long *haaaah* sound.

2 Take 2 or 3 breaths here at your edge, and with each out breath, let the stretch happen just a tad more. If it hurts, then back off a little. Don't strain; instead, allow the stretch to happen. Let yourself into the stretch, and let that breath just fall out. *Haaaah.*

3 Slowly release your arm and let it float down beside your body as you let your head float back to vertical. Take your time. There is no rush. Slowing down is important with these stretches. When your head comes back up, keep your eyes closed and take some more deep breaths as

you focus your attention on your neck—both the left and right sides. What do you notice?

Be aware of any tendency you have to push or force the stretch. Most of us come from a background in relation to any form of physical exercise that follows the "no pain, no gain" approach. That is not the approach to take with your yoga practice in this program. Here you are being asked to move slowly into and out of each stretch, taking your time to find your edge and making it an edge that you can sustain for 3 or 4 slow, deep breaths as you focus your awareness. This approach is also likely to be different from what you might find in some yoga classes that are more focused on physical achievement than on the deeper aspects of yoga. If you take a little time to master the technique of these stretches, the benefits of the Phoenix Rising approach will be greater and will come more quickly.

4 Now for the other side. Let your head fall a little to the right. Place your right hand up over your left ear and use the weight of that arm to slowly draw your head a little farther until you feel a stretch on the left side of your neck. Try to coordinate any movement toward or into the edge with a long exhale.

It is the slow and long exhaling of the breath that issues an invitation to the body to perform the stretch in a way that allows rather than forces it to happen. Practice it. Wait for the exhale to move toward the edge, and take several breaths to find it. Once at the edge, take 3 more long, slow breaths before slowly releasing your arm and letting

your head float back up as your arm floats down. Take another deep breath and notice what's happening now. Just notice.

With this approach, you should always take at least a 15-second pause between one posture and the next. Take that time, but instead of counting seconds, count breaths. Some time during this first week, take a clock with a second hand and see how many long, slow breaths you take in 15 seconds. The longer and slower your breath, the fewer breaths you'll take in that quarter minute. As your body grows more accustomed to this technique, you may take only 1 or 2 breaths every 15 seconds. Whatever the number is for you, use it during that time between one posture and the next to count your breaths before moving on.

After the neck stretch to each side, we do a shoulder shrug.

5 Bring your shoulders up toward your ears. Slowly squeeze them a little higher, but not too high. Find your edge. Take a few breaths as you hold the shrug.

Try holding the last breath in for as long as you can while still holding the shrug. Then let the breath fall out as you release the shrug. Pause for the several deep breaths that you do after each posture as you also focus your awareness and notice what is happening. Then repeat the shrug one more time, again holding the last breath as you hold the shrug. Pause again after you release it.

Three-Part Breath

Next is a breathing exercise. As you may have noticed, working with breath both in the postures and separately is something we give a lot of attention to in this program. Have you ever compared how you breathe when you are tense with how you breathe when you are relaxed? In these cases, the breath responds to what is going on in the body. Did you know that the opposite is also true? The breath can be used to create different states of being in the body just as easily as it responds to them. If you can master this technique, you can change the way you feel in just a few minutes by breathing a certain way.

I call this exercise "Three-Part Breath" because it focuses on breathing to three parts of your body as a way of helping you deepen your breath. As you learn to breathe more deeply and fully, you'll find it easier to use a deep breath whenever you need to relax a little. Here's how to do it.

1 Stand with your feet planted firmly on the floor about hip width apart, your spine long, and your arms by your sides. As you take a short breath in, lift your arms directly out in front of you to shoulder height, palms facing down. Hold the breath in.

2 Take a little more breath in as you sweep your arms out to the sides of your body, keeping them at shoulder height with palms facing down. Continue to hold the breath in.

3 Now take a third breath in as you raise your arms above your head, bringing the palms to face each other. Hold this breath for a moment or two and then let it go as you slowly lower your arms out to the sides and down. So what you have done is inhaled 3 times before exhaling. The inhales can be short and quick, but the exhale needs to be long and slow.

4 Now there is one more thing to add to the practice. With each inhale, you will focus on sending your breath to a different part of your body. With the first breath in, imagine it is going all the way down to your belly. With the second, imagine it is filling the bottom part of your chest. And with the third, see it filling your upper chest all the way to your throat. It's as if you are progressively filling up the front of your body from the groin up in 3 separate breaths. If you practice this daily as part of your routine, it won't be long before you notice your breathing deepening and slowing down, even when you are not trying to deepen or slow it. In time, this will have a profound effect on how you experience your life. For now, just do it. Repeat the practice 4 times and then notice what happens while you are doing it and while you pause between rounds and before the next pose.

Swinging Twist

This next exercise is meant to be done with a "let loose" approach.

1 Stand with your arms hanging loosely by your sides, your feet planted firmly on the floor a little wider than hip-width apart, and your knees slightly bent.

2 Take a deep breath and let it fall out. (Notice we do that a lot and always at the beginning and end of a posture or an exercise.) Begin to swivel from your hips—to the left as far as they go and then back to the right as far as they go. Continue this slow movement left, then right, and as your hips swivel, let your arms begin swinging in the same rhythm and direction as your hips, wrapping around your body as they go.

3 Bring the breath into the exercise by letting out a loud *haaaah* as you fully exhale every time you end a swing to the left or right. (Notice that you are being encouraged to make noises in your yoga practice. Sound is a perfectly natural accompaniment to body movement and particularly to anything you are doing that helps you to release any tension that your body may be holding. So go for it. Make noise. This is another good reason to have a place in your home that is private—where you can close the door and do your thing without any outside interference and without bothering anyone else, either.) So you are now swiveling your hips left

and right, swinging your arms across the front of your body on each swivel movement, and letting out a loud *haaaah* with each out breath every time you swing one way or the other.

4 There is one more thing to do: As you swing, also follow the movement with your head, turning it all the way around to the left as you swing left and to the right as you swing right. Look back into the far corners of the room behind you and see how far around you can look each time. This brings your neck into the exercise along with your torso. What is great about Swinging Twist from a physical perspective is that it rotates your whole spine on its axis from the pelvis all the way up to the neck. However, this means you need to be cautious and not get too wild or push too hard with the movement. Remember, maintain a "let loose" attitude. Continue for about 20 complete rounds and then take another 4 or 5 swings to bring the motion to a stop. End by standing in stillness with your eyes closed. Observe your breath, your feelings, your thoughts, and so on.

Side Bend (Half-Moon)

1 Stand with your feet close together and bring your arms up over your head, joining your hands together and making a "steeple" with your index fingers. Straighten your arms as much as possible and lengthen your body from the hips so your spine is long and straight but not strained. Take a deep breath in. On the exhale, reach with your fingers out to the left to point them toward where the wall and ceiling meet, but don't stretch yet.

2 Take another breath, and again on the exhale, move a little farther out to the left. Take another breath, and this time find your edge for the posture. You will probably feel the edge on the right side of your body. Find an edge that you can sustain for a little while. More resistance would be too much,

and less resistance would not be enough. Find that just-right place for you and breathe deep falling-out breaths. *Haaaah*.

3 Hang out there at the edge for 3 or 4 more full breaths. While you are there, tune into the sensations in your body, your feelings, your thoughts, and anything else that is happening for you. There's no need to fix or change what is happening, no need to make it go away. Just

be with it. Notice it. Watch it. Experience it fully.

4 On the next inhale, move back to an upright position, drawing your arms up above your head, and exhale as you lower your arms back down to your sides. Pause for a few deep clearing breaths and again notice what is happening. There are two parts to every posture: the engagement and the release. Always be present to both, paying attention

what you experience moment to moment when you are in the posture, on the way out of it, and just out of it.

5 Inhale as you raise your arms above your head again and repeat the sequence on the right side. Remember to take 3 breaths to find your edge. There is no rush. You will find that if you sneak up on the edge rather than rushing to it, the posture will work much

better for you and you will get more from it. Also remember to move out toward the edge only on the exhale. It's your body's signal to say yes to the posture.

6 When you find the edge on your reach to the right (the stretch will most likely occur on the left side of your body), hang out for 3 or 4 more deep letting-go breaths. *Haaaah.* Remember, sound is okay. Again watch what happens at the edge. Don't anticipate what will happen; just be open to whatever does happen. Getting used to doing your yoga practice in this way is what is going to change your experience of life in time. So embrace it. Be the one who watches, notices, and experiences sensations every time you engage in a posture. Stay with it on the way out and for a few breaths after that, as well.

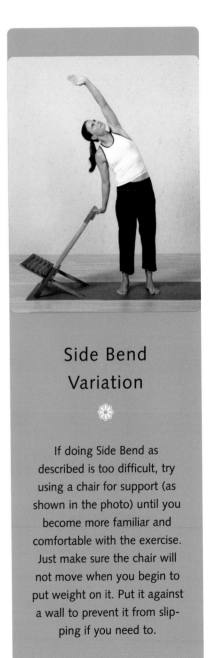

Side Bend Variation

❀

If doing Side Bend as described is too difficult, try using a chair for support (as shown in the photo) until you become more familiar and comfortable with the exercise. Just make sure the chair will not move when you begin to put weight on it. Put it against a wall to prevent it from slipping if you need to.

Back Bend

1 Stand with your feet planted firmly on the floor, hip-width apart, and place your fists behind your back just above your waist, with the flat part of your fists pressing up against the large muscle that runs beside your spine.

2 Bring your elbows as close together as they will go behind your back. Engage your pelvis by pressing it forward a few inches in front of you and at the same time look up toward the ceiling to open your throat and chest. Take a deep breath and let it fall out. Continue to take deep breaths and let yourself a little farther into the back bend on each exhale. Find your edge. Here at the edge, make sure you can still take deep breaths. If your breath is constricted in any way or you are feeling as if you are struggling for breath, you have gone too far. Back off a little to the place where you can breathe fully, and once full breaths are established, you can test again to see if you can go farther into the edge.

3 Stay in the back bend for 3 or 4 deep breaths, and while there, bring your focus to the front side of your body. As you focus there, notice what is happening for you: body sensations, feelings, thoughts, images, or whatever. Slowly stand back up, release your arms to your sides, take a deep breath, and continue to notice what is happening.

Emotions on the Mat

Sometimes in a posture such as this, you may experience feelings that are not familiar to you. This is perfectly fine and part of the process of using your body to learn more about yourself. If this happens, simply continue to breathe and notice what is happening. Don't try to push the unfamiliar feelings away; instead, let yourself experience them. Different people experience different things in yoga postures. There is no way of knowing or predicting what you'll experience. You may have read elsewhere about attempts at labeling postures to go with certain feelings or states of being. Although some people may experience similarities when they perform the same postures, I prefer to treat every yoga posture I ever do as a totally new experience with new things to be discovered. I avoid trying in any way to script or set up that experience beforehand. Think of it like the weather. It changes daily. So do you. So what you experience today might be quite different from what you experience tomorrow. Moreover, your body has a wonderful intelligence of its own, and it will give you the experience you need when you need it and when you can handle it. It won't take you to places you shouldn't be going. So trust it and be open to whatever it gives you.

Having said that, I do know from my own experience and from working with others that for some people, a back bend like this one will produce feelings of vulnerability. You are opening up your front side (often thought of as the vulnerable side) and exposing it as you bend backward, which leaves you with little in the way of quick protection from any threat coming toward you. So what do you do if you feel vulnerable in this or any other posture? You may be inclined to try to shift the posture in some way to get rid of that feeling, and that is understandable. Why feel vulnerable? If you do that, however, you will miss out on the chance to learn more about your vulnerability—and yourself in the process. Just as there is a physical edge in every posture, there can also be an emotional edge. I invite you to watch for these emotional edges. They won't occur in every posture, and you might not notice them at all until you have been

continued on next page >

practicing daily for several weeks, and maybe not even then. We learn about ourselves in a variety of ways. But if a feeling does come up, try to go to the edge with it. Find a place in the posture where you can simply be present to whatever the feeling is. Let's say it is a feeling of vulnerability. Go with it and let yourself feel it as fully as you can. It may be accompanied by a few tears or another body sensation, such as a lump in the throat, a sinking feeling in the stomach, or a change in body temperature. This is a normal part of the process of yoga and not something to fear once you've let yourself experience it a few times and begin to realize that it can actually be very helpful and healing.

I used to feel vulnerable every time I did a particular back bend. At first it was almost unbearable because it was a feeling that I wasn't used to experiencing. Over time, as I let myself feel it as fully as I could and played the edge with it, it began to become less intense and easier to be present to. One day, I noticed there was no more vulnerable feeling. In fact, what I felt instead was a feeling of strength. By accepting my vulnerability, I became stronger. I also noticed that around that same time, a similar process was occurring in my life as a whole. As I began to allow myself to be present to some vulnerable areas that I had previously avoided and became more accepting of myself as a result, I became a stronger person in many ways. So whenever you encounter an unfamiliar feeling in any posture, know that you can use your yoga experience to explore this feeling and in the process find out more about yourself, possibly transforming some aspect of your life by doing so.

Back Bend Variation

❁

If you have difficulty with Back Bend as described, you can use this variation until you feel more comfortable with it. It requires the use of a prop or support, such as a chair or table. Make sure that it won't slip and that it is sturdy enough to support your weight. To start, simply stand with your back to the chair or table and place your hands on the top edge of it about shoulder width apart. As you take your grip, just lean back and use the support to steady yourself. Adjust your feet (usually by walking forward a few inches) so that you find your edge in this modified back bend. Let your head fall back and open your chest as far as you can to keep a safe edge. Then follow the directions for Back Bend.

Standing Forward Bend

After Back Bend, your body will most likely want to go into a forward bend to counter the back stretch. I like to notice this desire coming from my body and follow it from one posture to the next. This yoga sequence was designed in part to follow the natural flow from one posture to the next.

1 From your standing position after Back Bend and after taking at least 1 full clearing breath, gently allow your body to begin a forward move by bending from the hips, not the waist. A good way to do this is to imagine that you have a swivel that goes from one hip to the other. Then imagine you are bending from that swivel and allow your upper body to bend forward over your lower body.

2 The first part of Standing Forward Bend should be a "letting go" posture. Bend the knees a little to make it easier to move into a forward hang. Just hang like a rag doll and let your whole upper body go loose. Let your arms, head, and torso be heavy and hang with no effort needed. Let your jaw hang, too, with your mouth open.

3 Take some deep breaths in and let them out through your open mouth with a *haaaah*. Notice if other sounds want to emerge, as well, and let them.

continued on next page >

Most of the postures in this sequence could be classified as either postures that engage your body or postures that do the opposite and invite your body to surrender. The first part of Forward Bend—the rag doll part of it—is one that invites surrender. Don't think of surrender as a bad word. To some of us, it may imply giving up or being weak. I prefer to think of it as letting go. It is an opportunity to let go of what you are holding on to in your body and in your life. In order to be present to life these days, most of us require quite a bit of effort and vigilance. We have to be alert and awake in order to navigate all the little and big challenges that we are called upon to face in many moments of our day. Our bodies and our minds get used to being in this "forever ready to engage" mode. A balanced life has both times to engage and times to let go. Just as the tide has an ebb and a flow, so does a balanced life. So in our yoga practice, we make room for both of these aspects of life. Notice if you seem to prefer one over the other. It's okay if you do, and in time, by simply noticing that preference, you will learn more about yourself and the balance that you are creating or not creating in your life. This in turn will give you the chance to choose to make some changes to create more balance. There is no need to rush this process. The reason this program is designed to be done over 8 weeks is because it takes about that long for most of us to get what we need from it.

The second part of Forward Bend calls for you to go from a state of surrender to a state of engagement.

4 Grab your ankles or heels if you can reach them. Tuck as much of your forearms as you can behind your calves and bend your knees enough to allow your head to touch your knees or get as close as it can to them.

5 Begin to straighten your legs by pulling with your arms to create a stretch on the back side of your body (usually the hamstrings). As you do with all other postures, take your time to sneak up on the edge and find that place of not too much and not too little. This is one of the most difficult postures in this routine in terms of being able to find your edge.

6 After 3 or 4 deep breaths at the edge, release your grip on your ankles and once more come to the surrender part of the posture by allowing your body to just hang forward, letting go of all effort and allowing your breath to be deep and to fall out.

7 Then bend your legs a little at the knees and begin to roll up slowly to standing. As you roll up, imagine that you are stacking each vertebra of your spine on top of the one below until you reach a straight standing position. Breathe and notice what is happening now: body sensations, feelings, images, anything at all—just notice.

A hamstring stretch usually produces a sharp edge, and it's easy to go too far too soon and meet your resistance very quickly. It's also a difficult posture in which to sustain the hold at your edge. Again, resistance tends to kick in. I once taught yoga in a special school for troubled teens. One of my students told me that every time he did this posture, he felt as if he wanted to run out of the room. With my help, he was able to notice this feeling when it came up and to simply "be with it" as he breathed deeply into the edge. In time, he began to see how in life he would often habitually run away whenever he encountered resistance. By the end of the yearlong yoga program, he told me he was able to learn how to "be with" and embrace his resistance in life, as well as in Forward Bend, rather than reacting to it.

Forward Bend Variation

Use the same prop—a chair or table—that you used in the Back Bend variation. Reach forward and let your body hang but be supported by your hands on the chair or table in front of you. For the surrender part of the posture, bend your knees slightly so that you can just hang in a relaxed way without any stretch.

For the engagement of the posture, straighten your legs while at the same time straightening your arms by walking back a little from your support to stretch your hamstrings. You may notice a stretch around your shoulders, as well. Follow the same directions as in Standing Forward Bend for playing the edge and coming out of the posture.

TRANSITION TO FLOOR

You are now going to come from your standing position to a position facedown on your mat. It's a good idea to have a small, clean hand towel where your face will rest.

During your yoga and meditation practice, there will be many points of transition. A transition is moving from one posture to another or one position to another. Instead of just changing positions quickly and without paying attention, try using all your transitions as opportunities to practice mindful awareness. As you move from one posture or position to the next, do so with focus on what you are doing and notice what happens. Do you tend to want to rush the transition? Or do you take your time?

Paying attention to the transitions in your yoga and meditation practice will help you become more aware of the transitions you make every day in your life. Someone I know always used to be late for appointments. He was late because he never allowed time for transitioning from one activity to another. At an unconscious level, he had difficulty accepting that transitions take time. When he began to pay attention to how he made transitions in his yoga practice, he became aware of his tendency to rush and ignore the move from one thing to the next. It was as if he didn't want it to be there.

You may think I'm spending time talking about something that is minor and perhaps not very important. Although it may appear that way, I can assure you that for some people, paying attention to transitions can have a huge impact on their lives. In my friend's case, he now shows up on time, allows space in his daily schedule to move from one thing to the next, and actually enjoys the time between one activity and another. The stress level in his life is less than half of what it used to be just because he pays attention to transitioning and allows time for it. Try it as you move from standing to lying facedown on the floor.

Half Facedown Boat

1 Rest either your chin or forehead on your mat. Straighten out your arms on the floor above your head. Bring your awareness to the left side of your body. Completely ignore the right side for now.

2 As you focus on the left side, begin to lengthen it by stretching your left arm and left leg along the floor away from the center of your body. Imagine the left side getting about 4 inches longer at each end. Don't forget to breathe as you do this. As with all stretches, let this one be accompanied by deep, long, slow inhalations and falling-out exhalations. After you have lengthened the left side, also lift your left arm and leg a few inches off the floor as you keep your focus on this left side. Pay attention to what is happening as you lengthen and lift a few inches. Go as high as you can to sustain the position for 3 or 4 deep breaths without struggling.

continued on next page >

If you ever find yourself struggling with a posture, it usually means you need to back off a little. Find a place where you can sustain the posture with what I like to call "effortless effort." In other words, some effort is involved and you do know that you are working, but it's work and effort that you can handle. It's not the kind of effort that makes your whole body want to scream, or the kind that forces you to quit or run away. Instead, it is effort that can be sustained and also allow you to focus on the subtleties that are occurring in your body and in your whole being as you do the work.

3 As you hold this long and lifting stretch on the left side of your body, what do you notice? Check in with your body and any sensations, feelings, and thoughts. Perhaps you can even notice a particular "personality" that appears in this left side of your body—a certain feel, character, or quality. Whatever it is, just notice it. No need to do anything with it or explain it. Now take another full breath and then slowly transition by letting your arm and leg come back to the floor and by turning your head to a comfortable position. But for a moment or two more, keep your focus on the left side. Continue to notice what is happening during this release phase of the posture.

4 Transition your focus from the left side to the right side. Notice what happens as you do so. It may take a little internal effort to shift your focus and bring awareness to the right. Accompany the shift with a slow, deep breath.

5 As you focus on the right side, repeat the practice that you used on the left. Rest either your chin or forehead on your mat, straighten out your arms on the floor above your head, and maintain awareness on the right side exclusively. Then stretch your right arm and leg along the floor, imagining that this side of your body is getting a few inches longer at each end. Follow this by lifting your right arm and leg a few inches off the floor, as well. Focus awareness on what is happening here on the right side, looking especially for a feel, quality, or character. Hold for 3 or 4 full breaths and once again release back to the floor while continuing to pay attention to the right side during the release.

What did you notice? Was there any difference between the left side and the right? (There is no correct answer to that question. Some people notice a difference, and some do not.) If you did notice a difference, what was it? Is there any connection between what you noticed in your body and what you notice in your life? Asking this question will sometimes provide new awareness about yourself. Be careful, though, of inventing answers to this kind of question. If something is there to be noticed, then notice it, but there is no need to fabricate a feeling. You will have many opportunities to increase your awareness of yourself as you go through this practice daily for 8 weeks. On some days, you will notice things that will dramatically increase your knowledge of yourself. On other days, you may not notice much at all. Moreover, some postures will produce more awareness than others at different times. This is to be expected. We are all different, and each of us is different on every day of our lives. Nothing is ever the same.

Cobra

Cobra is a classic yoga pose and one of my favorites. It offers the opportunity to be present to yourself in a whole new way. Again, remember you only need to go as far as you can for as long as you are able to with each of these poses. Do not interpret my directions here as the law. You may need to modify them to suit your body, and this is perfectly fine.

1 After the Boat posture, bend your legs at the knees and let your legs flip-flop from side to side like a pair of windshield wipers. This is a great way to release any residual "holding on" in your lower-back area before you move on to the next posture.

continued on next page >

2 Place your hands under your shoulders with your palms facing down. Feel the mat with the flattest part of both your hands and let your fingers be long and slightly spread apart. Rest your forehead or chin on the mat and tuck your elbows in close to your sides. Take a deep breath. (This posture is one to enter and leave slowly. Transition between each movement by pausing to take a deep falling-out breath.) Begin by lifting your head a few inches off the floor. Breathe. Then lift your chest a few inches. Breathe again. Begin to focus on your hands and let them take a little of your upper body's weight as you lift your chest a few more inches. Breathe. Lift your head to open up your throat. Breathe.

3 At this point, your belly button should still be in contact with the floor. Now you have a choice. Stay at this place in the posture and continue to breathe and notice, or let yourself a little farther into the posture by extending out from your lower back and placing a little more weight on your hands as you come up a little higher. Breathe deeply all the while.

4 When you arrive at your place in the posture, hang there for 3 or 4 breaths if you are able to. As you do this, notice what is happening. What quality does this posture bring to you in this moment? To fully get the feel of this posture, I suggest imagining that your chest is being drawn forward in front of you. Imagine the center of your chest moving out ahead of you and leading your body. This allows a lengthening feeling to come from your lower back, so rather than scrunching up your back as you bend upward, you are extending your back out from your pelvis.

5 Just as you took your time to enter the posture, take your time to release it. Pause a few times on the way down to take a deep breath. When you finally reach the mat again, let yourself melt into it, releasing your hands and arms to a comfortable position by your sides and turning your head to where it also feels comfortable. Continue to breathe and notice. What is happening now? Watch, feel, experience, and be present to each moment as you are present to yourself in it.

TRANSITION TO BACK

Roll over onto your back. Transition with awareness, taking time to focus.

Knees to Chest

1 Once on your back, wrap your arms over the tops of your knees and pull your bent legs in toward your body. Imagine you are giving yourself a big hug. What is that like? What do you notice as you hug yourself? Can you say quietly to yourself, "I love you"? What happens if you do? Just notice. Again, there are no right or wrong answers.

2 Take a few deep breaths as you squeeze your knees up to your chest. Then release your grip and extend your legs out along the floor again. Pause for a few breaths, letting your belly rise with each inhale and fall with each exhale as you let your body be heavy.

Here is something to reflect upon as you give yourself a hug. This body has been everywhere you have in every moment of your life. When you've had to run, it has helped. When you've had to fight and take a stand, it has helped. When you've been sick and had to heal, it has joined in and helped. Every time you have celebrated, it has been involved in expressing joy through laughter. Whenever you've been sad or hurt, it has felt your pain and shed your tears. Every step of the way, it's been there.

Corpse

Some say this is one of the most difficult yoga postures. This is not, of course, because of any physical difficulty but because of the difficulty of being able to really "play dead" with nothing happening—a complete letting go. Here are a few ways to help you get there.

1 Lie flat on your back with your arms by your sides, palms facing up. Imagine that your body is very heavy. Follow your breath in and out, letting your belly rise with each inhale and fall on the exhale. You might want to imagine that you have a large, flat, and heavy stone on your belly. As you breathe in, the stone rises, and as you breathe out, it falls. Do a quick scan of your body and notice any areas where you are holding tight. Breathe to those places and invite them to be heavy. Imagine that you have nowhere to go, nothing to do, and nothing worth thinking about except being heavy and just letting go. Notice what happens. Let go some more. Notice again, and so on.

2 Stay here for a few minutes. As you practice more, you may realize that you can reach a state that is somewhere between awake and asleep. You are not asleep, but you are in such a deep state of letting go that you are not really awake, either. Don't worry if that is not happening now. You may find that your mind is still busy or you are fidgety or have feelings that emerge. This isn't bad. In fact, it's very good. It is your body's way of bringing issues to your awareness. Resist the temptation to solve anything for now. If you slip into problem-solving mode, simply notice that you've done that and come back to your breath and being present to whatever it is you are noticing. There's no need to do anything else. Just keep noticing and letting go, letting go and noticing.

Transition from Yoga

This ends the physical part of your practice. After your few minutes in Corpse pose, draw your knees to your chest and engage in a rocking motion that after 2 or 3 backward and forward rocks brings you up to a sitting position. Find a comfortable position to sit in for a few more minutes.

Meditation

In this program, you will be doing a lot of sitting. If you look at pictures of people practicing sitting meditation or yogis in sitting positions, you will most commonly see them in what is known as the lotus position, with legs crossed in front and feet resting near or on top of the thighs. This looks great, and to someone who has been doing it for years and has open hips and knees, it can be quite comfortable. For most of us, though, this isn't the case. By all means, spend a little time trying it each time you practice, but when it gets to the "ouch" point, select a more comfortable sitting position. I have had people go through this entire program using a chair every time they were sitting. Some of them got as much or more from the program as the adept yogis who sat in lotus every time. It's more important for you to position yourself to be able to focus than it is to adopt any particular sitting technique. Being a very pragmatic yogi, I say you should do what works best for you and don't sweat the small stuff. The essence of the program and staying with it each day are important. How you sit is small stuff!

So for 5 minutes, in whatever is your comfortable sitting position, simply be with yourself and your body and watch the activity of your mind. Observe and be a witness to yourself. Then take a few deep breaths and follow the directions for your integration of the day's experience.

Body Scan Meditation Exercise

In the early part of the program, I am going to offer you a very easy way to begin your meditation practice. You are going to do it lying down. How about that! No difficult sitting position; you'll just lie flat on your back for about 15 minutes or so. You will use your body as an anchor to help you focus.

1 Lie down on your back and make yourself comfortable and warm. You may want to put a pair of warm socks on your feet, cover yourself with blankets, or use blankets to support your legs, neck, or head.

2 Once you are comfortable on the floor, notice the parts of your body that are in contact with it. Feel your body being supported by the floor. Close your eyes.

3 Become aware of your breath without changing it or judging it. Notice your abdomen rising on the inhale and falling on the exhale. Allow your breath to support you in becoming aware of your body as you embark on a journey through the body, being present to whatever is happening moment to moment, with no need to fix or change anything. If your mind wanders, simply notice it and come back to the breath. Use the breath to bring your awareness back to the body.

4 On your next exhale, bring your attention to the toes of your right foot. Notice whatever sensations reside in your right toes. Notice if there are no sensations. If you come across any sensations, stay there, present to them, and breathe. Come back to your breath; notice the rise and fall of your belly as you inhale and exhale. On your next exhale, become aware of the top of your right foot. Notice any sensations. Notice if there are no sensations. Every experience is valid. Nothing is right, nothing wrong. Send your breath into the sole of your right foot. Notice whatever is there. If your mind wanders, simply notice it and bring your attention back to the breath and to the sole of your right foot. Continue to move your awareness up your right leg, piece by piece, pausing to identify and breathe to your right ankle, shin, calf, knee, thigh, and finally your whole leg.

5 Repeat the process for the left leg, beginning with the toes and working your way up, piece by piece, breathing into each body part and noticing. Each time your mind wanders, gently bring it back to your body and your breath.

6 After you breathe into your whole left leg, take a moment to notice any differences between your left and right legs. Notice the different sensations. Notice similar sensations. Come back to your breath.

7 On your next exhale, bring your awareness to your right buttock. After a few breaths, shift to your left buttock. In turn, direct your awareness to your lower back, then the middle of your back, your upper back, and your shoulders. Then move on to the front side of your body: Go to your pelvis, then your abdomen. Next, focus on your chest and your heartbeat. Breathe and notice. Each time you wander, just gently come back to your body and breath.

8 On your next exhale, bring your attention to your right shoulder; then move to your right upper arm, elbow, lower arm, wrist, hand, and fingers. Breathe into your whole right arm. On your next exhale, let your breath travel to your left shoulder; then repeat on the left side: upper arm, elbow, lower arm, wrist, hand, and fingers. Send your breath into your whole left arm. Become aware of any different sensations in your left arm compared with your right. Notice the similarities.

9 Bring your awareness to your throat, then to your neck, chin, jaw, cheeks, ears, nose, eyes, area around the eyes, forehead, top of your head, and back of your head. Don't rush. Spend at least 1 or 2 full breaths at each location.

10 Become aware of your whole head and then your whole body. Breathe in and out to your whole body. For variation, try breathing in through the front side of your body and out the back for a few breaths. Then imagine breathing in through the soles of your feet and out through the crown of your head. Finally, try directing the breath in through your left hand and out through the right. Take a few more moments to just be with your whole body—letting go and letting it be.

11 Start to move and stretch gently. Bend your legs and roll onto your left side. Use your arms and bring yourself up to sitting.

12 Reflect on what you noticed. Log in your journal anything you noticed as you went through the practice.

Walking

This week, you are asked to take two 10-minute walks as part of your practice. Try to include each walk as a part of your 40 minutes for the day rather than scheduling it separately. There is a reason for this. The walk is a little different from what you would normally consider a walk. It's a kind of walking meditation and is practiced in much the same way (with conscious awareness) as the rest of your daily practice. So it's better if you do it in the same time frame.

Set aside any additional clothing you might need for your walk the night before so you won't have to waste time looking for a coat or a sweater when it's time to hit the road. On the day of your walk, take your watch and time 5 minutes out (away from your house) and 5 minutes back. Walk at a brisk pace but one that you can easily handle. As you walk, breathe deeply and feel your whole body. Notice your feet hitting the ground, the swing of each leg as it comes forward, the swing of your arms, the fullness of your chest, and the length of your spine. Be with your body as you walk. Feel it. Notice it. Breathe to it.

If the weather outside is anything less than a blizzard or a tornado and you are in a reasonable state of health, go for your walk. Take an umbrella if it's raining, take water and walk slowly if it's hot, dress warmly if it's cold, but don't let the weather stop you. My children's school requires the kids to spend at least some time outdoors at recess time, regardless of the weather. The school maintains that such a practice supports the educational and health goals of the curriculum. The children are more alert and focused than they would be if they were to remain indoors for the entire day. So try it. See what happens for you.

Integration

Reflect on your practice today. What happened for you? What did you notice about yourself and how you related to yourself as you practiced? What was your main awareness coming out of this practice today? Just notice that.

Now ask yourself this question: "Was there any connection between any awareness that I had and my way of being in my life?" Just answer the question to yourself honestly from a place of being a detached observer. At this stage, you are not solving problems but becoming aware of yourself.

Next, try to connect with the part of you that is your own best friend. Imagine that a very wise and all-knowing person dwells somewhere inside of you. This all-knowing person is there to look out for you, to love you, to take care of you, and to give you advice that will be in your best interest. Take a few quiet moments to visit with this wise one and ask for guidance: "Given what I've become aware of here in my practice and how it connects to my life, what do I do with that? What's my next step? What is it that I'm being guided toward in my life, and what am I leaving behind?" Let the answers come from the inside. Avoid making anything up, and accept whatever you get. It may be words, or it could be a feeling or an image of yourself. Whatever it is, just receive it and notice it. And let it be. Take the last few moments to let your inner wisdom affirm you. Here you are doing something to enhance your life. That is important and commendable. Every time you practice, let your inner guide affirm you for making the effort, for taking the time, and for committing to living a life that is more conscious and in tune with the wonderful being that you are.

Journaling

Every day, take 5 minutes to write in your journal about any awareness you received during your practice and how it connects to your life. Also write about

any guidance you may have received when you tried to connect with your own inner wisdom. At first, you might not be sure that you are receiving any guidance from within, and you may have doubts about it if you do. This is normal. This program is based on many different ideas that may seem strange to you in the beginning. One of those ideas is the belief that each and every one of us knows what is best for our lives. It's as if each of us has a compass that points to the direction that we need to take at any given time. At different times in our lives, the direction will be different for each of us. No two of us are identical, so adopting other people's answers to our life questions is usually not a good idea. We need to find our own answers and learn to trust our own knowledge of what is right for us. If we haven't been doing this in the past (and I would say that is true for most of us), we need to learn how to do it. It takes some practice and patience, and at first the direction or guidance we get may be a little vague or unclear. It helps if you look for the essence of the direction you are being guided toward rather than the details.

I remember a particular time in my life when I had been spending most of my days working and taking care of my family, and I received in my guidance an image of myself as a young child sitting on top of my father's shoulders at a street carnival. For a moment, I experienced the fun, excitement, and sense of awe I must have felt at that time. It was a signal from my voice within to create more of that in my life. I wasn't having much fun at that time, and I needed it.

Now, that didn't mean I had to become a 6-year-old boy again or even have fun in the same way that he did. But it did lead me to explore what would be fun for me at that time and how I could responsibly build that into my life. I believe any life change must be handled responsibly. We all have commitments and people in our lives who depend on us in some way. If we make big changes, we need to take into account the impact that such changes may have not only on us but on others, too. This should not be a barrier that prevents us from changing, but it may mean we need to go about change in a particular way. For me, having more fun meant taking a few hours each week to hang out at the local airport and talk with fellow pilots about flying, one of my main recreational pursuits. When I did that, it was like a time-out for me from my busy world. I could just blow off a couple of hours and feel good about doing something that I might otherwise have put aside to take on some other so-called important task.

Sometimes your journal might take the form of a sketchbook or even a scrapbook. One of my clients used to browse magazines after her yoga therapy session to find pictures that represented, or were in some way connected to, the guidance she had received. Her journal became a collection of images and words from magazines that offered her a reminder of the direction she was now choosing for her life.

This week in your journal, take some time to record how you are doing with befriending your body. What is it like? What happens when you do it? What are you learning about yourself as you do this?

Drinking Water

Most of the time when we decide to make changes in our lives, this involves not doing the things that we know harm us—eating junk food, smoking, and the like. In this program, particularly in the early stages, we don't want you to quit anything. Instead, just do the program as outlined and begin to add some good things into your life. One of these is drinking 8 glasses of water per day. Not too difficult, you just have to remember to do it.

Drinking water helps to hydrate your body and expel toxins from vital organs. As you begin to practice yoga, even in this early stage, your body will begin to discharge built-up toxins. Water is needed to help the process. On top of that, if you drink 8 glasses of water daily for a week, you might notice that you just plain feel better. Because this is easy to do and generally has a very positive result, it's part of this program. Try it and see what you notice.

Putting Intention into Action

This and every other week of the program, as you begin to become more aware of yourself and how you are showing up in your life, you will have the opportunity to try out new ideas that come to you during your practice—particularly in the integration exercise at the end of each day's practice. See if you can find ways to put new awareness to work for you in your daily life. It may be as simple as deciding you want to smile more or pay a compliment to a loved one or give your child or partner a hug. Simple things such as this may not look like life-changing acts, but if you repeat them and practice them with conscious awareness, they will go a long way in supporting you as you turn your stress into bliss.

Taking a Bubble Bath

For some folks, this is not something new. But even if you've taken many bubble baths in your life, you'll benefit from this one. And if you are new to the bubble-bath experience, you are in for a treat. For some unknown manly reasons, I used to believe that activities like this were not for me. I've changed my mind about that. Anyone can enjoy soaking in a deliciously hot tub of bubbles.

As you do with everything else in this program, you need to take your bubble bath with conscious awareness. Also try to fit it into your 40-minute practice time rather than scheduling it separately. It's part of the practice of making friends with your body by doing something good for it. Really feel that water and the bubbles. Let yourself into the bath gently and let out a long, slow *haaaah* sound in appreciation of the sensation of sinking into it and letting go as you do. As you sit, simply allow yourself to be there. You have nothing else to do and nowhere else to go. Just sit and enjoy.

WEEK TWO

Congratulations! You have completed the first week of your program and are about to begin the second. How did it go? What do you notice about yourself after 1 week? Are you any better friends with your body? Are you finding it easy or difficult to find the 40 minutes each day? Is there any strategy you need to employ this week to make it easier? Remember, the program works best if you take it one day at a time. For today, simply make the firm commitment to be there for yourself for that 40 minutes tomorrow. And then tomorrow make the same commitment for the next day.

This week, the theme is becoming more aware. Now, you might wonder why you would want to do that. Or you might argue that you are already aware. The truth is that most of us most of the time live in a state of selective awareness. We are aware of the things that support life the way we have set it up, and we selectively hide from our awareness of the things that might rock the boat and cause change in our lives if we were to be honest with ourselves.

For example, at one point in my life, I smoked 30 or more cigarettes a day. (I'm pleased to say that more than 25 years have passed since I quit.) At that time, however, I was not aware of the extent of my habit, its control over me, my reluctance to do anything about it, or the damage it was doing to my body. Sure, I kind of knew in the back of my mind that it was not good for me, but each time I took a drag, I quickly and easily pushed that thought away. I did not want my awareness of that action to get in the way of a habit I enjoyed.

Another big area of our lives in which we often put our awareness aside is our relationships. Are we really conscious of what we are doing when we react to something our partner or one of our coworkers might say to us? And what about our relationship with the food we eat? Do we bring awareness to the act of eating, or is it just an unconscious act that happens periodically throughout our day?

Awareness is the first step toward change. Without it, we are usually going nowhere. But becoming aware is tough. If we are prone to getting down on ourselves, we have another great reason to avoid awareness. Who wants to spend half the day beating himself up for all that he is noticing? So rule number one for practicing awareness is to put away the "stick." I'm talking about the imaginary stick you might use to beat yourself up with when you come across something about yourself you don't like. Also, practicing awareness is not only about noticing the things you don't like. It's also about noticing all the great moments in each day. We are often only selectively aware of those, too.

Practicing awareness demands that we slow our pace a little. If we are rushing from one thing to the next, we have little time to become aware of what is really happening at any moment. Try taking a sip of water slowly enough to notice the taste before you swallow it. This takes only an extra moment but will give you a whole new perspective on a simple sip of water. Apply that same practice of awareness to other moments in your day. How do you sit while eating? How do you stand while brushing your teeth? The list could go on and on.

For this week, we'll keep it simple. Try to focus your awareness on three areas: your body, your breath, and your thoughts. Check in with your body periodically during the day. How does it feel in the moment? How are you holding it? Where does it feel good, and where does it not feel so good? How about your breath: Is it deep and full or shallow and rapid? And what are you thinking about? Check in with your mental process from time to time. Notice what you spend your day thinking about. Do you have a thought that seems to keep coming up during your day?

Focusing on your body, breath, and thoughts is also the concentration for your yoga and meditation practice this week. As you go through your 40-minute routine each day, bring your focus to the same three things during every part of it.

It is said that there are basically three kinds of people in the world when it comes to awareness. There are those who are asleep and don't know they are asleep. Let them be. And there are those who are awakening but don't know it. Stir them gently. Finally, there are those who are awake and know they are awake. Take good care of them. They are the guides for us to follow. In this program, I am not asking you to wake anyone up other than yourself. So if you've been asleep for a while in terms of your self-awareness but know you are awakening (this is likely the case, or you would probably not have picked up this book or read it this far), then stir yourself gently.

Week Two

Set aside 40-45 minutes each day to practice.

Su

SUNDAY

Body, Breath, and Thoughts—Focus and Intention Setting: **2 minutes**

Yoga Practice Sequence: **28 minutes**

Meditation and Integration: **5 minutes**

Journaling: **5 minutes**

* Take at least five 20-second awareness breaks today
* Drink 8 glasses of water today
* Perform 1 small act today to support your intention
* Schedule a treat for your body for later this week

M

MONDAY

Body, Breath, and Thoughts—Focus and Intention Setting: **2 minutes**

Sitting Meditation Exercise: **15 minutes**

Walking: **15 minutes**

Integration: **3 minutes**

Journaling: **5 minutes**

* Take at least five 20-second awareness breaks today
* Drink 8 glasses of water today
* Perform 1 small act today to support your intention

T

TUESDAY

Body, Breath, and Thoughts—Focus and Intention Setting: **2 minutes**

Yoga Practice Sequence: **28 minutes**

Meditation and Integration: **5 minutes**

Journaling: **5 minutes**

* Take at least five 20-second awareness breaks today
* Drink 8 glasses of water today
* Perform 1 small act today to support your intention

W

WEDNESDAY

Body, Breath, and Thoughts—Focus and Intention Setting: **2 minutes**

Sitting Meditation Exercise: **15 minutes**

Walking: **15 minutes**

Integration: **3 minutes**

Journaling: **5 minutes**

* Take at least five 20-second awareness breaks today
* Drink 8 glasses of water today
* Perform 1 small act today to support your intention

Th

THURSDAY

Body, Breath, and Thoughts—Focus and Intention Setting: **2 minutes**

Yoga Practice Sequence: **28 minutes**

Meditation and Integration: **5 minutes**

Journaling: **5 minutes**

* Take at least five 20-second awareness breaks today
* Drink 8 glasses of water today
* Perform 1 small act today to support your intention

F

FRIDAY

Body, Breath, and Thoughts—Focus and Intention Setting: **2 minutes**

Sitting Meditation Exercise: **15 minutes**

Walking: **15 minutes**

Integration: **3 minutes**

Journaling: **5 minutes**

* Take at least five 20-second awareness breaks today
* Drink 8 glasses of water today
* Perform 1 small act today to support your intention

Sa

SATURDAY

(If you have already completed 6 days this week, then this day is optional. If you don't want to practice, spend an hour doing something you really love to do.)

Body, Breath, and Thoughts—Focus and Intention Setting: **2 minutes**

Yoga Practice Sequence: **28 minutes**

Meditation and Integration: **5 minutes**

Journaling: **5 minutes**

* Take at least five 20-second awareness breaks today
* Drink 8 glasses of water today
* Perform 1 small act today to support your intention

Body, Breath, and Thoughts—Focus and Intention Setting

When you are ready to begin your practice, take 2 minutes to focus your attention on your body, your breath, and your thoughts—the activity in your mind. You can do this while sitting on the floor or standing—however you feel most comfortable at the time. Knowing that it is sometimes difficult to get started, I will often vary the position I use to begin. I allow myself to be in whatever position feels good for the first few minutes of my focusing and intention setting.

After you have spent a few moments focusing on and noticing your body, do the same with your breath and then your thoughts. You don't have to do anything with what you notice, and remember rule one: no stick.

After this, set your intention by asking yourself, "What is it I'm hoping to create in my life by doing this practice today?" After a while, you will get used to this little daily exercise. It might seem simple, yet it is very important. It's a way of connecting what we are doing to what we are wanting. And we do this one day at a time. Notice that the question is about today, not next week or next year. Yes, those bigger and longer-term intentions are also important, but for now, let's just look at today. What do you want to create in your life today, and how will this 40 minutes you are about to commit to yourself help you?

Yoga Practice Sequence

This week, your yoga routine is basically the same as last week's except for one change at the beginning and for the focus of awareness you will be applying as you practice.

You will start your practice with Standing Body Scan. This is similar to the body scan you did last week during your meditation practice, but it is done standing up and has a slightly different focus. It is an excellent way of practicing awareness. It's also a great way to keep you connected to your body.

The time allotted for your yoga practice in this second week has been increased to 28 minutes. This is to allow you to move a little more slowly though the routine and to stay in the postures a little longer as you focus on breath and awareness. Here is the complete yoga routine for this week:

1. Standing Body Scan

2. Falling-Out Breath/Stillness

3. Neck and Shoulder Stretch

4. Three-Part Breath

5. Swinging Twist

6. Side Bend (Half-Moon)

7. Back Bend

8. Standing Forward Bend

9. Half Facedown Boat

10. Cobra

11. Knees to Chest

12. Corpse

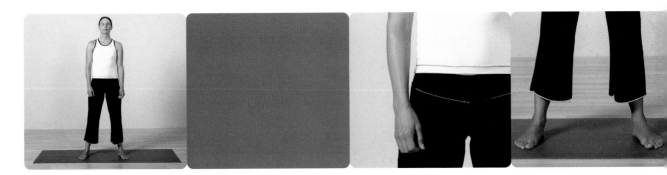

Standing Body Scan

As the name implies, Standing Body Scan is usually done in a standing position, but if you are new to yoga or can't stand for 5 minutes or so, you may use a chair.

1 Close your eyes and take 3 or 4 deep breaths that fall out on the exhale. Then direct your attention to your feet and hold your focus there for a few breaths. Notice your feet. There's no need to judge, explain, fix, or do anything about what you notice.

2 Bring your awareness to your ankles and do the same thing: Focus there for a few breaths. Then move up the legs to the calf muscles and lower legs. Focus and notice. Go to the knees and focus there. Then move to the thighs—the inside, outside, front, and back of each one. Notice and be present to this part of your body for a few breaths. Move to the pelvis. It's like a bowl, with your groin as the bottom and your waist as the top. Focus on this pelvic bowl for a few breaths. Move your awareness to your belly. Be present to your belly. Just notice it. Also notice if at any time you are thinking certain thoughts or feeling certain feelings—positive or negative. There is no need to do anything with the thoughts or feelings or even chase them away. Just notice them and move to the next part of the exercise.

3 Move up to your chest and notice it as you breathe. Experience it fully for a few breaths. Then place your attention on your shoulders. Notice your shoulders in relation to the rest of your body. Breathe. Move the focus to the neck and head. Which part of your neck is holding your head up right now? Just notice that. Which way is your head wanting to move even though it's still? Notice that.

4 For a moment, focus on the whole front side of your body, then the whole back side. Notice the parts of your body that seem to want to move forward. Notice those that seem to want to go back. There is no right or wrong here. There is no need to fix or adjust. Just notice.

5 Now imagine that a line is dividing your body into two halves: a left half and a right half. Take a minute or two to focus on just the left half of your body. Go there and be present to this side of you. Notice it and notice the feelings, sensations, textures, sizes, colors, shapes, and even sounds on this left side. Again, there's no need to change anything. Simply notice.

6 Move the focus from the left side to the right side by taking a deep breath and letting it fall out as you transition. See what you observe on this side. You may not notice all of the things on the list above. That is fine. Notice whatever you can.

7 Take another deep falling-out breath and then for the last minute of this exercise, take a moment to thank your body. Thank it for all that it has done for you in life. Thank it for being here for you now and for being the home of the life that is inside of it—this life that is yours. If you have difficulty thanking your body, that's okay. Just notice that and be aware of it. The important thing is to attempt to follow the directions and to notice your own response to that effort. There is no right or wrong response.

Every time you do Standing Body Scan, you will most likely notice different things. This is normal. The key part of this and all future scans of your body is your attention. Make it as focused as possible. This exercise is to help you begin to notice as much as you can about yourself, and this will carry over into all other areas of your life as you practice it more often. Watch and see. You won't experience that, however, until toward the end of the 8 weeks. So even though it may not seem as if much is happening at this stage, hang in there. Like most good things we do in life, this program takes time to have an effect.

After the scan, you are ready to engage your body in some yoga stretches and breathing exercises. Follow the remainder of the Week One yoga sequence as outlined above. As much as you are able to, allow your inner dialogue to focus around becoming more aware. As you do each posture, notice everything, but in particular, notice your body, your breath, and your thoughts. Ask yourself at least once in the engagement part of each posture, "What's happening now, body? What's happening now, breath? And what's happening now, thoughts?" And notice without needing to edit or make anything different. Whatever the awareness, it is what it is.

Meditation

This week on Monday, Wednesday, and Friday, you will begin a 15-minute sitting meditation exercise. As the focus for this week is awareness, you will simply be sitting for the allotted time and watching your body, your breath, and your thoughts. On the days when you are not performing the 15-minute sitting meditation (now through the end of this program), you'll meditate for a few minutes before your integration practice. The process is the same no matter how long the meditation session lasts.

Find a way to sit that is comfortable for you. You might want to experiment with different sitting positions on different days. If you need support for your

back and need to be elevated a little so you can more easily bend your knees and relax your body, try sitting on a firm pillow with your back against a wall. Using a chair is fine, too. Make sure you will be free of interruptions. Turn off the ringer on the phone, close the door to your room, and do whatever you have to do to guarantee yourself some quiet time.

When you practice sitting meditation, you may notice yourself drifting—falling asleep, going off on a train of thought, daydreaming about the future, or reliving a story from your past. If you notice yourself drifting during your meditation, just say to yourself, "I'm drifting," and let this acknowledgment bring you back to watching your body, your breath, and your thoughts.

Walking

On the days you practice sitting meditation this week, you will also take a 15-minute walk. And yes, maybe you guessed that while you are walking, you are still practicing watching and becoming aware of your body, your breath, and your thoughts—except when crossing busy roads, that is. You may need to shift your mind-set about walking to get the most out of this part of your program. This walk is not just for exercise, although certainly that's a big benefit of it. Brisk walking, even for only 15 minutes, 3 times a week, will make a difference to you physically if you have been sedentary for a long time. But it has the potential to do a whole lot more if you also make it a part of your meditation practice by walking with awareness. As you walk, watch your thoughts, notice your body, feel your breath. And just as you did in the meditation part of your practice, if you notice yourself drifting, simply say to yourself, "I'm drifting," and gently come back to what is happening for you in the present.

After your walk, don't forget to rehydrate your body with water. Aim to drink 8 glasses today and every day this week.

Integration

Ask yourself, "What did I notice today in my practice? In particular, what did I notice about myself? Do I see any connection between what I am noticing about myself and how it shows up in my life?" Take a moment to connect to the wise part of yourself, the part that knows you and loves you no matter what. Ask that part of yourself for guidance: "What could I learn from what I am noticing? How could I use what I am learning to make a change in my life that would serve my best interest?"

Journaling

This week in your journal, make sure to record any new observation that comes to you from practicing being more aware. What do you see now that you didn't see before? What are you noticing about yourself? What else are you noticing? Also record any guidance you receive during your integration.

Awareness Breaks

During the day this week and in subsequent weeks, you are asked to take some 20-second awareness breaks. An awareness break is simply stopping what you are doing or thinking or saying or being for 20 seconds and using that 20 seconds to notice what is happening to you and around you. It's very easy to do and yet potentially very powerful. If you are not by nature an inward-looking person, I suggest you try going inward with your awareness breaks. Try being very present to yourself and what is happening for you. Notice your feelings, your thoughts, and your state of being. That's all; just notice. If, on the other hand, you are very self-aware but tend not to see what is going on around you, you can choose to use your awareness breaks to focus more on what's happening out there in your world. Don't take your awareness breaks only at work. Try some at home, too.

I stumbled across this practice many years ago, and it has had a profound impact on my life. It was introduced to me as the spiritual practice of inward and outward meditation. The disconnection between the two didn't make sense to me, so I modified the practice to make it fit more easily into my daily life. Once while returning home from a teaching trip of several days, I took a 20-second pause before opening the door of my house. I learned something about myself that to this day has changed my life immeasurably. I saw my anxiety in those 20 seconds—my concern about how I would find things when I walked in. What might be out of place? What could have gone wrong? What household chores were not done? As I saw all this in my thoughts, I noticed a question: "Is this how I want to be as I walk into my house and see my partner and children whom I've missed so much while I've been away?" Then I noticed how quickly that question became an intention. I took a breath, felt the love for my family that was lurking underneath my fears, opened the door, and embraced the first person I saw with a big hug. My homecomings have never been the same since that day. They are now always full of love and celebration, as I've made that the first priority after walking in the door. Sometimes I have forgotten, but I've noticed that, too, and then returned outside for a moment before reentering after a 20-second awareness break.

In case you missed it, the most important aspect of this story is my taking the time to become aware. Without that 20 seconds of empty space, I would not have seen the loaded thoughts and the fears they were propelling, which in turn were affecting my behavior. As a result of taking the time to become aware, I could change my habitual behavior and create a different life outcome. I had the power to create what I wanted in my life, but only after I had become aware of what I had been creating and compared that with what I wanted to create.

Use your awareness breaks in a variety of places and at different times of the day. Try one as you look in your closet, as you sit in your car, before you pick up the phone, as you sit at your computer, and so on. Awareness is the first step to change, and a most important one. That is why it is the theme for this week and something that will continue to have emphasis throughout this 8-week program.

A Treat for Your Body

This week and for the remainder this program, make sure that on Sunday you schedule a treat for your body for later in the week. This is something that is in addition to your regular program time, and it can take as little as 10 minutes or as long as you want. For example, you may want to go and get a 1-hour massage or hike a mountain or kayak down a river. It should be something that you like and that will give you a genuinely relaxing experience. Schedule it for a time that works best for your personal calendar.

WEEK THREE

The theme for this week is *acceptance*. Last week, we practiced becoming more aware. Now it's time to learn how to accept whatever awareness comes to us.

Practicing acceptance does not mean that you are surrendering to the status quo and not going to change anything. It simply means you are accepting what is, as a precondition to change. In our modern world, we are always trying to change things—to make things bigger and better, to solve problems, to fix what doesn't work properly. This focus on change also finds its way into our personal lives. We often look outside of ourselves for some way that will make a difference and make our lives more pleasant. When anything we stumble across offers even the slightest possibility of improvement, we rush to grab it and incorporate it into our lives. Sometimes we get lucky and find something that really does work. More often, however, we come up empty and continue to look for the next thing that will fix whatever needs to be fixed. The steps of becoming aware and then learning to accept what we have discovered about ourselves are often not part of life's process. These steps take both time and self-inquiry. It is easier to skip these steps and rush for the first possible solution that appears on the horizon. So in this program, you are being asked to avoid doing that and to take time to engage in self-inquiry and the acceptance of whatever you discover about yourself as you inquire.

In my 20s, I was fortunate to live in a part of the world few people even today get to visit. I was teaching at a college in the city of Port Moresby in Papua New Guinea, a small island country north of Australia. Diversity and acceptance were an essential part of the culture there, where hundreds of different tribal groups cohabited and spoke more than 700 languages. One thing I noticed was the slowness in decision making among some of the traditional villagers with which I visited after being invited by my students. Sometimes it would take many days to decide something that on the surface seemed quite simple, like whether to agree to a marriage union between two people or not. As I observed more closely, I noticed that the villagers participated in a lot of discussion around such events that was all about familiarizing themselves with what was really happening (becoming aware) and taking a lot of time to literally sit with a decision before making it (acceptance). I also noticed that once a decision was made, even though it may have taken several days, there was often a

unanimous voice around it and a huge commitment to following through with it. Little did I know that in the next stage of my growth, as I embraced the Eastern practices of yoga and meditation, I would see a link to the primitive culture of Papua New Guinea in terms of how such practices actually worked in a real-life way.

In saying this, I am not suggesting that slow decision making is always the right way. There are certainly times in life when quick decisions and fast action are both important and necessary. When I fly an airplane, I don't "sit with it" when receiving instructions from air-traffic control. At the same time, if I'm thinking about my relationship with one of my children and what action to take in response to something that has happened, I may be well served by taking a few days to sit with it before responding or, worse yet, reacting. Most of us are good at making the quick response. Our schools have generally not prepared us very well for sitting with a decision. So in this program, we will learn this in the form of practicing acceptance.

When applied at a personal level in response to something you have discovered about yourself, acceptance can be quite humbling. It may mean getting comfortable with being imperfect (which all human beings are, believe it or not). I remember in the early days of my yoga practice, as I focused more on what was happening moment to moment, I discovered some hidden anger and frustration lurking in the awareness of myself. As I sat with it more and accepted it more, I discovered that I was often angry with people (particularly my children) at times because I somehow felt powerless to have them comply with my wishes for how they should show up in the world. Amazingly, as soon as I was able to accept that this was so and to sit with it, the feelings seemed to disappear. From that moment on, the more I was willing to accept myself as a less-than-perfect parent, I was able to accept my children as being less than perfect. Then later, I was not only able to accept these little oddities about myself and others but also to celebrate them as part of the wonderful tapestry of being human.

What If I Can't Accept?

You may have already asked that question, and if you haven't, I can assure you that if you follow the guidance on practicing acceptance this week, there will be a time when this question arises. You will probably come across a particular awareness that you don't feel you can accept or even just let be. What do you do with that? Well, the answer is simple: Just notice yourself not being able to accept. That is part of your reality, part of your awareness of self, and like everything else, it can be accepted also.

Your program this week is similar to what you did last week, with a few minor variations to fit the theme of acceptance.

Su

SUNDAY

Noticing and Accepting—Focus and Intention

Setting: **2 minutes**

Yoga Practice Sequence: **28 minutes**

Meditation and Integration: **5 minutes**

Journaling: **5 minutes**

* Take at least five 20-second awareness breaks today
* Practice accepting all that you notice
* Drink 8 glasses of water today
* Perform 1 small act today to support your intention
* Schedule a treat for your body for later this week

M

MONDAY

Noticing and Accepting—Focus and Intention

Setting: **2 minutes**

Sitting Meditation Exercise: **15 minutes**

Walking: **15 minutes**

Integration: **3 minutes**

Journaling: **5 minutes**

* Take at least five 20-second awareness breaks today
* Practice accepting all that you notice
* Drink 8 glasses of water today
* Perform 1 small act today to support your intention

T

TUESDAY

Noticing and Accepting—Focus and Intention

Setting: **2 minutes**

Yoga Practice Sequence: **28 minutes**

Meditation and Integration: **5 minutes**

Journaling: **5 minutes**

* Take at least five 20-second awareness breaks today
* Practice accepting all that you notice
* Drink 8 glasses of water today
* Perform 1 small act today to support your intention

W

WEDNESDAY

Noticing and Accepting—Focus and Intention

Setting: **2 minutes**

Sitting Meditation Exercise: **15 minutes**

Walking: **15 minutes**

Integration: **3 minutes**

Journaling: **5 minutes**

* Take at least five 20-second awareness breaks today
* Practice accepting all that you notice
* Drink 8 glasses of water today
* Perform 1 small act today to support your intention

Th

THURSDAY

Noticing and Accepting—Focus and Intention Setting: **2 minutes**

Yoga Practice Sequence: **28 minutes**

Meditation and Integration: **5 minutes**

Journaling: **5 minutes**

* Take at least five 20-second awareness breaks today
* Practice accepting all that you notice
* Drink 8 glasses of water today
* Perform 1 small act today to support your intention

F

FRIDAY

Noticing and Accepting—Focus and Intention Setting: **2 minutes**

Sitting Meditation Exercise: **15 minutes**

Walking: **15 minutes**

Integration: **3 minutes**

Journaling: **5 minutes**

* Take at least five 20-second awareness breaks today
* Practice accepting all that you notice
* Drink 8 glasses of water today
* Perform 1 small act today to support your intention

Sa

SATURDAY

(If you have already completed 6 days this week, then this day is optional. If you don't want to practice, spend an hour doing something you really love to do.)

Noticing and Accepting—Focus and Intention Setting: **2 minutes**

Yoga Practice Sequence: **28 minutes**

Meditation and Integration: **5 minutes**

Journaling: **5 minutes**

* Take at least five 20-second awareness breaks today
* Practice accepting all that you notice
* Drink 8 glasses of water today
* Perform 1 small act today to support your intention

Noticing and Accepting—Focus and Intention Setting

This week, as you begin your daily practice, take a few minutes to focus on acceptance. Do this by first focusing on your body, noticing it, and accepting it just the way it is. Do the same with your breath and whatever else you are noticing about yourself as you begin your practice. Also take a moment to bring to your awareness what it is you want to create in your life by spending this time today. Set your intention.

Yoga Practice Sequence

Your yoga practice this week follows the same sequence as it did in Week Two, beginning with Standing Body Scan. This body scan is included again, as it follows on with the themes of awareness leading into acceptance. In the scan this week, as you become aware of each area of your body, use it as an opportunity not only to deepen your awareness of self but also to practice accepting it just as it is—perfectly imperfect. Apply the same approach with all of the postures in your yoga routine. Notice the places where you struggle, and accept the struggling. Notice the places where you drift, and accept the drifting. Notice the areas of your body that you like and don't like, and accept the liking and not liking. Do the same for anything else that you notice.

Meditation

Use your meditation this week to practice acceptance. Accept any thought you notice. Accept any drifting into your past or future. A little trick you can use to help with practicing acceptance as you meditate (and in your yoga, too) is to notice and then simply say to yourself, "Aah…and it is so," and exhale as you do.

Walking

During your walks this week, you have another great opportunity to try on acceptance. Surely you will notice things on your walk. Perhaps it'll be the traffic, or something a dog left on the sidewalk. What opportunities to notice and accept. "Aah…it's traffic. Aah… it's dog shit. Aah…and it is so." And don't leave yourself out just because you are noticing what is on the external. Whatever you notice about yourself, accept it. As you watch your thoughts during your walk, you may notice that what you see on the pavement is symbolic of some of the stuff that is in your mind, and accepting it can be quite freeing. "Aah…thoughts about xxx. Aah…bullshit. Aah…and it is so."

Integration

In your integration this week, bring to focus what you are noticing, what you can accept, and what is difficult for you to accept. See how this connects to your life. Seek guidance from within about it. Ask your inner guide, "What actions could I take that might make a difference?"

Journaling

This week, make the focus of your journal writing your awareness of yourself around the theme of acceptance. "What can I accept about myself? What is difficult to accept? What guidance did I receive about this and how might it apply to my life?" Record anything else of importance that you notice either during your practice or in the rest of your day.

Awareness Breaks

Continue to use your 20-second awareness breaks (at least 5 each day) and take an extra few seconds to practice accepting the awareness (or acknowledging the difficulty in doing so).

WEEK FOUR

You will now begin to notice the benefits and changes of the program. Your body will begin to feel different because of the yoga practice, and you will also notice that your thinking and your way of being in the world will start to shift. At first, the changes will be subtle and barely noticeable. Then one day, you will simply become aware of not doing the same things the same way anymore. One participant in one of our live programs who had been a chronic worrier came along in the fourth week and said that he was still a worrier but that now when he worried, he noticed it, and when he noticed it, he was able to laugh about it. Now, on the surface, that may not seem like a lot, but to him, it was awesome. His worrying no longer had a grip on him and his life. Before the program, he would worry a lot about his body and how he felt. As a result of his yoga practice, he had many times in each day when he actually felt good in his body. This new evidence of his body experience meant that when he worried about his body, he could actually check in with it and see how it felt rather than just continuing to worry as he did in the past.

Of course, if you are at this point in the program but haven't been very consistent with your daily practice, then you most likely won't notice any changes yet. If this is the case, what do you do? Do you quit? Do you recommit and start getting with the program from here on? Do you go back to Week One and start over? Really, the choice is yours. The neat thing is that you can start again anytime you want. With this book as your guide, you can do your program on your terms. You can cheat if you want. You can skip days or even weeks. It's your program. All I can tell you is that I know that it will produce noticeable benefits for those who follow it. I don't know what it will do if you only partly follow it. You might get some benefit, and you might not. It's your decision as to how much benefit you want to achieve. Keep in mind that it's not a bad thing to need to recommit. It's a part of life. We all make commitments we find difficult to live up to from time to time, but if we know they are commitments that are in our best interest or that we really want to keep, then we recommit. We start over and do what we originally intended to do. Just remember the advice at the beginning to commit for one day at a time and to be sure to make that commitment every day.

So, are you ready to move on to Week Four? It's interesting that in the above paragraph, I asked you to examine what choices you might be making about your commitment to this program, because the theme for Week Four is choice.

When we begin to become aware and when we are then able to accept that awareness, we arrive at a point of choice. You could argue that this point could arise without the awareness and the acceptance, and this may be so. Choices are available in every moment. But are they real choices? Or are we driven by habitual reactions at times rather than considered choices? How often do we choose to do what seems like the quickest and easiest way to get around an issue or problem, only to find that once again it doesn't work? How many failed relationships result in new relationships that also fail? How many diets and exercise programs fail time and time again? How many vacations or nights on the town or any other form of escape we may choose still leave us with that empty feeling at the end? If our choices are not supporting us in creating what we want in our lives, then perhaps we are not arriving at genuine choice points in our journeys. Perhaps we are making habitual or expedient choices, but just like the mouse in the maze, we keep going up the same tunnel and finding no "cheese." We go up

the same tunnel because it's what we know, what is familiar, and what appears safe and dependable. Maybe there have been some signs of cheese from time to time—a few fleeting moments of pleasure, the promise of better things to come—but at the end, still no cheese.

To make the kind of change in our lives that will really make a difference, we must learn to make choices that will support our getting to the cheese. Knowing what the cheese is for us will help. At the start of this program, and each day when you set your intention, you are making a statement to yourself about what cheese in life you are seeking. Then as you engage in the program and follow the directions for each week, you begin to notice things about yourself and increase your awareness of them. You also have the opportunity to accept these things. Perhaps this is valuable information about yourself and may explain your propensity to look for cheese where it isn't, if you tend to do that. If you follow the steps in the integration part of the program, you may receive further insight into what is being revealed to you, and you may even arrive at a new choice point. You can continue to do what you've done in the past, or based on your new awareness, you can choose to do something different.

Choice is powerful. It means we can move in new directions and bring about real change. When we discover genuine choice points, we often face a temptation to want to change everything right now. So here is a word of caution: Move slowly and carefully, and begin with just one or two new choices in the way you live your life. Take the time to feel the impact of a new choice before making too many more. After all, you need to know the new choice is really working, and to do that, you need to test it for a time. Also, there is no such thing as a right choice or a wrong choice, a good choice or a bad choice. There are only consequences or results produced by a following a particular choice. This is an important distinction and one worth remembering as you begin to walk the path of choice.

Of course, what will be helpful in making new choices is becoming more aware of choices you are currently making. So part of your practice this week will be to discover them by being more aware as you engage in your program each day and as you engage in your life each moment of the day.

Again, your program this week is very similar to the previous 2 weeks but with a focus on the theme of choice.

Week Four

Set aside 40-45 minutes each day to practice.

SUNDAY

Noticing, Accepting, Choosing—Focus and Intention Setting: **2 minutes**

Yoga Practice Sequence: **28 minutes**

Meditation and Integration: **5 minutes**

Journaling: **5 minutes**

* Take at least five 20-second awareness breaks today
* Practice accepting all that you notice
* Notice also what you are currently choosing
* Drink 8 glasses of water today
* Act on a choice today that will support your intention
* Schedule a treat for your body for later this week

MONDAY

Noticing, Accepting, Choosing—Focus and Intention Setting: **2 minutes**

Sitting Meditation Exercise: **15 minutes**

Walking: **15 minutes**

Integration: **3 minutes**

Journaling: **5 minutes**

* Take at least five 20-second awareness breaks today
* Practice accepting all that you notice
* Notice also what you are currently choosing
* Drink 8 glasses of water today
* Act on a choice today that will support your intention

TUESDAY

Noticing, Accepting, Choosing—Focus and Intention Setting: **2 minutes**

Yoga Practice Sequence: **28 minutes**

Meditation and Integration: **5 minutes**

Journaling: **5 minutes**

* Take at least five 20-second awareness breaks today
* Practice accepting all that you notice
* Notice also what you are currently choosing
* Drink 8 glasses of water today
* Act on a choice today that will support your intention
* Schedule a treat for your body for later this week

WEDNESDAY

Noticing, Accepting, Choosing—Focus and Intention Setting: **2 minutes**

Sitting Meditation Exercise: **15 minutes**

Closet Exercise: **15 minutes**

Integration: **3 minutes**

Journaling: **5 minutes**

* Take at least five 20-second awareness breaks today
* Practice accepting all that you notice
* Notice also what you are currently choosing
* Drink 8 glasses of water today
* Act on a choice today that will support your intention

Th

THURSDAY

Noticing, Accepting, Choosing—Focus and
Intention Setting: **2 minutes**

Yoga Practice Sequence: **28 minutes**

Meditation and Integration: **5 minutes**

Journaling: **5 minutes**

* Take at least five 20-second awareness
  breaks today
* Practice accepting all that you notice
* Notice also what you are currently choosing
* Drink 8 glasses of water today
* Act on a choice today that will support your
  intention
* Schedule a treat for your body for later this
  week

F

FRIDAY

Noticing, Accepting, Choosing—Focus and
Intention Setting: **2 minutes**

Sitting Meditation Exercise: **15 minutes**

Walking: **15 minutes**

Integration: **3 minutes**

Journaling: **5 minutes**

* Take at least five 20-second awareness
  breaks today
* Practice accepting all that you notice
* Notice also what you are currently choosing
* Drink 8 glasses of water today
* Act on a choice today that will support your
  intention

Sa

SATURDAY

*(If you have already completed 6 days this week, then
this day is optional. If you don't want to practice, spend
an hour doing something you really love to do.)*

Noticing, Accepting, Choosing—Focus and
Intention Setting: **2 minutes**

Yoga Practice Sequence: **28 minutes**

Meditation and Integration: **5 minutes**

Journaling: **5 minutes**

* Take at least five 20-second awareness
  breaks today
* Practice accepting all that you notice
* Notice also what you are currently choosing
* Drink 8 glasses of water today
* Act on a choice today that will support your
  intention
* Schedule a treat for your body for later this
  week

Noticing, Accepting, Choosing—Focus and Intention Setting

This week, begin in the usual way of breathing, noticing, and accepting what is happening in your body, your breath, and your feelings and thoughts. Then take it one more step: Choose how to be with that. Maybe you'll have to make a slight adjustment in the way you are sitting or how you are breathing in order to better support your intention. Become aware of that intention: "What am I doing here today? What am I wanting to create in my life? And how in this moment am I supporting that with the choice I am making right now?"

Yoga Practice Sequence

The yoga practice this week is the same as for Week One except you will be engaging in each posture for a slightly longer period to make the total practice time 28 minutes. In addition, you will substitute Wake-Up/Warm-Up Exercise from Week One for Standing Body Scan from Weeks Two and Three. The reason for this is to tune in to your body once more and notice the choices you make in each moment and where they come from. As you move from one position to another in this first series of movements, take the time not only to notice choice but also to explore it: "Do I choose to move quickly? Or do I choose to move slowly? Do I choose to hang out or move on? Where do I choose to go next? How do I choose to be with myself as I go through this series of nondirected movements? Where does the choice come from: my mind, my body, or somewhere else?"

Apply this same approach to all the other postures in your yoga practice this week. With each posture, as you notice and accept what happens moment to moment, also look for the choice underlying what is happening. It is amazing what you can discover by doing this. You may see tendencies that appear in your yoga practice that also show up consistently in your life. When I first began looking at choice as I went through my yoga routine, I was amazed to discover my propensity to choose to move on before I had taken enough time to just be present for a few more breaths with each posture. It wasn't that I was rushing my practice, but I was definitely choosing a less-spacious approach than I could have. I would want to move on, get on with it, and get to the end more quickly.

As I saw this tendency in my yoga practice, I also began to see it in my life. I could take a bath and enjoy it, but could I stay the extra few minutes and really soak in it? I could take time for a good meal, but could I chew slowly enough to really savor the taste? Needless to say, I could go on with a long list of all the things in my life that I chose to experience with a "not quite long enough" approach. This seemed to be a dominant choice in my life—the choice to move

on just a little before it was time. Just as I could describe a long list of areas where this choice showed up in my life, I could most likely write another book around the impact this awareness brought to my life when I began to explore some different choices in certain areas.

So this week, take the time to notice the choices you make moment to moment as you go through your yoga practice. See if there is a pattern or a dominant choice.

Meditation

In your sitting meditation this week, also focus on the theme of choice. As you watch your thoughts, see what choices go with them. See what you give attention to with your mind as you choose. Not surprisingly, when I did this, I became aware of how much of my thinking was future oriented. I noticed myself planning for the future more than dwelling in the past. To this day, I haven't really chosen to change this. My looking ahead is part of who I have accepted that I am and is a characteristic I want to keep. It supports my intention I wish to manifest in my life. By being more aware of it, though, I can be sure that this aspect of myself that I choose to accept and retain serves me instead of controlling me.

Walking

This week, there are only two walks instead of three; a new exercise (explained below) replaces the walk on Wednesday. During your walks on Monday and Friday, continue to notice and accept and also look at any underlying choices. Where do you choose to walk? How do you choose to walk? What do you choose to do while you walk? Again, no wrong answers, just information—and deeper awareness—to use as a basis for experimentation with different choices that support your intention.

Closet Exercise

Instead of taking a walk on Wednesday, spend the same time doing the following: Go to the top drawer of your dresser or the top shelf in your closet. Take a few moments to simply observe it. Notice all that you have chosen to store in this space. Notice how the items are arranged. Notice your response to the arrangement of the items. Just notice. And then accept it or notice that you can't. Close your eyes for a moment and breathe for 20 seconds, just letting it be. When you open your eyes again, explore the choices your closet reveals to you—choices you are making not only in relation to this closet but also to your life. How does my closet, in the way that I find it right now, reflect my life? How does it support or not support my intention? If I were to make changes to my closet, what would they be? How would these changes make a difference in my life? Remember, there are no right or wrong answers, just awareness and choice.

Integration

Ask, "What did I notice about myself during my practice today? How does this aspect of myself show up in my daily life?" Seek guidance from your inner wisdom about this awareness. Ask your guide, "What can I do with this awareness so that I might be able to live my life in a way that supports my intention? What is one small thing that I could do today that would begin to put into my life a positive way of moving in this direction?"

Journaling

Each day this week, journal the outcome of your integration along with anything else you are noticing. You may also want to record what happens when you begin to apply what you are learning about yourself by taking action in your daily life.

Acting on Choice to Support Intention

At this stage of the program, we are beginning to more consciously apply what we are learning about ourselves through our daily practices to our daily lives. This week (and in the weeks to come), you are asked to consider this by looking each day for a way to put intention into practice in daily life. Consciously

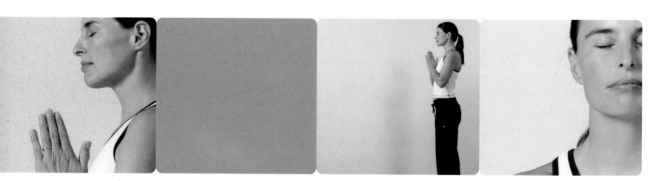

choose some small act that is easy to do but will make a little difference. Often the act you choose to follow will come from the integration exercise each day. Here is a simple example.

One morning as I was going through my yoga routine, I had a flash of myself some 20 years earlier. A very good friend came to mind—someone with whom I had spent many pleasant hours. My friend still lived in Australia, and I hadn't seen him for many years. I felt a sadness around that. In the integration part of my practice, I recalled this vision and feeling that had come up during my yoga. After asking how it connected to my life, I received this answer: "In my life, I want to have good friendships and close relationships. I want friends in my life just like my old friend Wally in Australia."

In taking the next step in the integration practice, I asked for guidance from my inner wisdom around this: "What do I do with this? How can I use this awareness in a way that will better support me in my intention in life?" The answer came quickly: "Spend more time with people you choose as your friends; take time to connect." I thought about that and then asked, "What can I do today to follow through on this guidance?" An idea came. One of my good friends is also my work colleague. She is always in the office before me each day, and when I arrive, we sometimes chat for a few minutes, usually about work-related issues. Our families have been friends for many years, and her grown daughters would often babysit for my children. I was aware that I hadn't seen them for a while or talked about them with Karen. So instead of talking only about work-related issues, I made the conscious choice to ask Karen about her girls—how they were and what they were doing—and to spend a few minutes chatting about them and feeling great about making the connection with her and with them through her.

It took a conscious effort, as I had become habitually in a hurry to get to my computer and get down to work, perhaps out of some fear that I would never have enough time to complete all I needed to in the workday. Noticing this made me more conscious of how I was often not allowing adequate time in my life to create what I wanted in terms of friendship. Good friendships don't just happen. You have to make space for them in your life. I had forgotten that. Many years ago, when Wally and I became good friends, we spent many hours together with no work agenda. We had time and made time to connect. Later that day, I also called Wally, and we chatted on the phone for an hour in a way that made the 13,000 miles and 20 years that had separated us seem insignificant.

As you read this, you may think this sounds way too simple. It may even appear trite. I can assure you, however, that it's the many little things we do or don't do in our lives that often lead us blindly into a life of more stress and less bliss. If we want to change that, it means becoming more consciously aware, or more mindful, of these little things. Many times, we have to learn all about ourselves again, particularly if we have lost touch with who we are, what we want in life, and what we are or are not doing to create it.

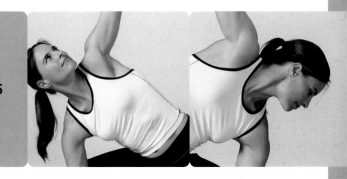

 Your One-Day Personal Retreat

THIS IS PROBABLY ONE THE MOST IMPORTANT AND MOST beneficial parts of this program. It is also one of the most difficult. It is so easy to skip this. There are so many good reasons why you cannot devote one whole 24-hour period of your life to nothing and nobody but yourself. That alone will bring up issues of "Am I worth it?" "Do I deserve it?" Then there will be the organizational issues: "What about my children, my family?" "What about all the chores that have to be done on the weekend so I can get to work on Monday?" and so on.

So go for it. Sit down with a pen and paper and write down all the good reasons why you can't make a 24-hour personal retreat for yourself happen. If you are game, read the list and then tear it up with the announcement to yourself, "I'm going to do it anyway!" Here are the steps to take to plan your retreat.

Choose a Date and Time

You should start planning your personal retreat day at least a few weeks ahead of time. You are looking for a 24-hour period. I suggest beginning in the early evening—say, around 6:00 P.M.—and going through to the same time the following day.

Choose a Place

You can do your retreat at home so long as you have the place entirely to yourself and let others know you will not be taking visitors. For most of us, this won't work. It is usually easier to find a place to go to. Make the choice a simple one. You are not going on vacation, so you don't need to fly to the Bahamas. Of course, if that is what will work best for you, go ahead. There are many retreat centers listed on the Web if you care to look in your area. These are often places where you can go for a make-your-own retreat. Sometimes they are yoga or meditation centers or monasteries that for a small fee or donation will allow you to come to their facilities for a personal time-out. You could also choose a small hotel or motel in a location where you can take walks and eat simply. You will need a room large enough and comfortable enough for your yoga mat and pillow.

Make Arrangements for Dependents and Pets

Make sure you cover all the bases with anyone or any pet for which you are responsible. This is very important. You need to be able to spend this 24-hour period as free of worry as possible about those you are leaving behind. Can you take your dog or cat? I would say preferably not. With a pet along, it is no longer a personal retreat. This is meant to be a time exclusively for you, with a minimum of interaction with anyone else. Most of us have never done anything like this before. I used to think it would not be something I would ever want to do; however, after I did it once, I was ready to do it again. Take my word for it that it is well worth the effort you need to take to make it happen.

Inform Someone of Your Plans for Emergencies Only

Let someone you trust know what you are doing and where you will be so you can be contacted if, and only if, an emergency arises. You might want to let others know what you are doing, but refrain from telling them where you will be or how they can contact you. They might think it's nice to call you in the middle of your retreat to ask, "How's it going?" This is not what you want to happen. There will be plenty of time after it is over to tell folks all about it if you want. If you are choosing to do your retreat at home, then you need to turn the phone ringer off and put a message on your voice mail that you are unavailable. Leave the number of a friend or neighbor who knows you are at home as an emergency contact if you must. Most important, though, is to set up your day so you will not be tempted to check voice mail or e-mail or any other kind of communication device. You need to be away from all of it for this single day.

Prepare for Celebration

Be sure to read the last section of this chapter, which gives instructions for the celebration that you will have at the end of your day. If it involves reservations or setting up a date with others, make those arrangements well in advance.

Let the Retreat Begin

So assuming you have made it happen, what are you going to be doing for this whole 24-hour period by yourself? The schedule below is written up as if your retreat will begin at 6:00 P.M. and end at 6:00 P.M. the following day.

Day Prior	**6:00 P.M.**	Arrive at retreat or settle in to being alone if you are at home
		Begin your 24 hours of silence
	6:00 – 8:00 P.M.	Eat a simple, healthy meal and take a long walk
	8:00 – 9:00 P.M.	Read over your journal entries from the past 4 weeks
		Reflect on what you read
		Write some more in your journal
Retreat-Day Schedule	**8:00 – 9:00 A.M.**	Eat a simple breakfast; shower and dress for the day
	9:00 – 10:30 A.M.	Yoga
	10:30 – 11:00 A.M.	Walking
	11:00 – 11:30 A.M.	Meditation
	11:30 A.M. – noon	Walking
	noon – 12:30 P.M.	Integration and journaling
	12:30 – 1:30 P.M.	Simple lunch and rest
	1:30 – 3:00 P.M.	Yoga
	3:00 – 3:30 P.M.	Walking
	3:30 – 4:00 P.M.	Meditation
	4:00 – 4:30 P.M.	Final exercise: integration and journaling
	4:30 – 6:00 P.M.	Celebration

The theme for your One-Day Retreat is your relationship with yourself (and others). By spending a complete day alone in silence, you will clearly learn much about your relationship with yourself. You will get to see how you interact with yourself through your thoughts and feelings, what tendencies and urges are present for you and perhaps driving you, what choices you make for yourself, and so on. Naturally, there will be a flow. You might also learn how your relationship with yourself carries over into your relationships with others.

One thing I noticed about myself was how demanding I can be of myself to do well and to complete and accomplish things. I noticed how I often expect similar things from my children, my partner, and my colleagues. This awareness is not one that I need to judge myself over. I just noticed it and am now more aware of how it shows up in my life from time to time. When I notice this tendency appear, I can now choose to allow it or to modify it. The awareness gives me more power over how I show up in my relationships with myself and others. See what you discover about yourself during this day. Also practice accepting whatever you notice, remembering that acceptance is an important step in the process of creating lasting change.

Following are details about the individual activities scheduled for your personal retreat.

Silence

You will be spending your 24 hours in silence. In case you don't know what that is, it means you don't talk to anyone about anything for any reason. Naturally, you will need to check in to your hotel if you choose to go to one, so do it before your start time. If you choose to eat in a restaurant during your 24 hours (it is probably better to take food with you), write your order on a piece of paper and hand it to the waiter while placing your finger over your lips to let the person know you are not speaking. He or she does not need to know the reason. If you feel compelled to communicate with anyone else, use the paper and pencil. Keep your mouth closed and let no words come from your lips during this time. If you break your silence by accident, notice what happened and simply resume it again.

During the whole 24 hours, you will be observing yourself as you go. One of the most striking things you will observe is what it is like for you to be in silence. Notice carefully. You will likely see things about yourself that you have

never seen before, like the need to explain yourself to people. The first time I was in silence and eating in a hotel restaurant, I felt I needed to explain myself to the waiter. Of course I didn't, and he was quite happy to read my order from the paper I had scribbled it on. It was hard for me not to explain myself, but he didn't seem to care. I immediately saw how in my life I have this propensity to want to explain myself to people. I probably waste a lot of my life energy doing it at times when it isn't even needed. I learned a valuable life lesson by noticing myself in silence. And this was not the only one. Numerous little gems came to me during this day, as they no doubt will for you. Remember, though, to just notice. There's no need to get down on yourself or fix everything in your life immediately. Simply observe and accept whatever awareness comes your way.

Eating

You can choose how to get your meals during this day, and I suggest you base your choice on what is the easiest way for you to take care of this bodily need. I used to advocate a modified fast during this retreat, but that does not work for everyone. If you can handle a modified fast, I suggest drinking lots of water and eating simple fruits, vegetables, and/or grains. The low-carb folks might want some lunch meats, cheeses, and low-carb snack foods.

Whatever or however you choose to eat, again practice observing yourself and your relationship to the food you eat during this day. Take a little extra time (you have plenty of it) to chew your food a little more, to notice the taste a little more, to swallow a little more slowly. You can use the act of eating as a form of meditation if you slow it down enough and notice as you eat. Above all, do not multitask while eating. No journal writing while eating. No walking while eating. Simply eat when it is time to eat. For some folks, this may be a new experience. Americans are known throughout the world for our capacity to do multiple tasks while eating. It almost seems to be part of the national character to be doing something else while eating. For some, the place where most meals are consumed is in the car while driving. I am not going to judge this strange behavior, but I'm one who prefers to sit for hours over a good meal and do little else but focus on the experience of dining. Regardless of your usual way of eating, during this retreat, place a little more exclusive focus on the act of eating itself, and observe. Notice how the experience this day connects with the rest of your life. Be aware and accept.

Journaling

Your journal is a key part of your One-Day Personal Retreat. On the first evening, you will read through your journal entries to reflect on all that you have observed in the past 4 weeks. It's also an opportunity to record any new observations or any overall awareness that comes from reading back over your entries. And think about what you want to get from this day. How is spending a day in silence by yourself going to support you in your life? How do you feel as you embark on this small journey in time? What feels good about taking this day for yourself? What are you afraid of? What do you think you will find difficult? Write down your answers to these questions and anything else that comes to you.

At a few designated times during the day of your retreat, you will write in your journal. During your time spent doing yoga, meditating, or walking, you will notice things about yourself. You will also most likely notice how these things show up in your life. These are important observations, often with life-changing potential. Make sure to remember them so you can record them in your journal at the times set aside for it. In some cases, you may have several hours of practice before getting to your journal. At each time scheduled for journal writing, take the time to reflect and recall anything of significance that you noticed along the way. As you observe what you are becoming more aware of, some questions may come to you, as well, and these questions might not have ready answers. If this happens for you, this is perfectly fine, and you do not need to answer the questions right away. Just record the questions for now. You may have to sit with them awhile before any answers appear. It is, however, important to know these questions are ones you are asking yourself.

The questions might be very deep or quite simple. Mine have ranged from "Do I need some new clothes?" to "Is being a good father to my children an essential and rewarding part of my spiritual practice?" Both of these had some life-changing answers down the road. So, whatever questions come to you, notice them, record them, and for now, just let them be.

Yoga

During your One-Day Personal Retreat, you will be doing a longer yoga sequence, but the approach you have been using is basically the same. The additional postures are described below, following the list for the longer sequence. This routine is one that you can use whenever you have additional time on any day of your program from here on out. If you take your time and focus on your breath as instructed, along with your inner experience and awareness, it will take you over an hour, and perhaps up to an hour and a half, to complete the sequence. In the second yoga session scheduled during your retreat, you will repeat the sequence, but of course your experience of it will be different. Notice the difference—physically and internally.

These longer sessions will give you an opportunity to go deeper into your yoga practice. Try holding postures a little longer, making sure you take full and deep breaths while doing so. Try relaxing into the postures at the edge. Be mindful of the notion of effortless effort. Use the posture as a place of exploration at the edge. Explore what is happening physically for you and also what is happening internally. Notice your feelings, your thoughts, any images that come to you, any memories of events long passed, and so on. Begin to use your body as a source of knowledge about yourself. Treat each posture as a totally new experience and be open to whatever you discover, regardless of how many times you may have performed that posture in the past and regardless of any previous experiences you may have had with it. If you can consciously do these things, your yoga will offer new and enlightening possibilities and will begin to serve you in guiding you in your life.

LONGER YOGA SEQUENCE

1. Focus and Intention Setting
2. Wake-Up/Warm-Up Exercise
3. Cat and Dog
4. Standing Body Scan
5. Falling-Out Breath/Stillness
6. Neck and Shoulder Stretch
7. Three-Part Breath
8. Swinging Twist
9. Heavy Bucket Swing
10. Squat with Breath
11. Side Bend (Half-Moon)
12. Back Bend
13. Standing Forward Bend
14. Warrior
15. Chair
16. Half and Full Facedown Boat
17. Bow
18. Cobra
19. Child
20. Knees to Chest
21. Bridge
22. Half-Seated Forward Bend
23. Full-Seated Forward Bend
24. Knees to Chest
25. Lying Twist
26. Corpse

Here are the descriptions for the new postures added to this sequence.

Cat and Dog

1 Get on all fours with your shoulders directly over your wrists and your hips directly over your knees. Your arms are straight, and your palms are firmly planted on the floor with fingers slightly separated. Your feet are hip width apart, toes pointing away from you, and your back is flat. Take a few deep and easy breaths.

2 On the next exhale, arch your back, bringing your chin toward your chest while shrinking your abdomen and expelling all the air from your lungs.

3 Momentarily hold the breath in Cat. Slowly inhale as you drop your belly toward the floor and lift your head to look up and sway your back. Hold the breath momentarily in Dog. Now slowly begin to exhale to Cat. Hold the breath momentarily and then inhale as you return to Dog. Repeat the sequence 5 more times. Slow down as much as you can to coordinate breath with body movement. Don't stress or strain, and maintain a stable base by keeping your arms and legs in alignment.

4 Return to neutral. Move to your feet and then stand up, allowing your upper body to hang down. Bend your knees slightly and then with a long inhale, slowly roll up to standing. Then exhale a long, slow breath. Stand and notice. What is happening now?

Heavy Bucket Swing

1 Bend from your knees and let your upper body come forward, reaching with your arms to pick up two imaginary heavy buckets of paint that are out in front of you. Inhale a deep breath as you lift the buckets high above your head and stand to your full height. Hold the breath in momentarily as you hold the heavy buckets above your head.

2 As you exhale with a loud *haaaah* sound, let the buckets drop and swing down and behind you as you bend your knees at the same time. Repeat by inhaling slowly and lifting the buckets above your head

again as you straighten your legs. Hold and then drop and swing through again, bending your legs as you do and letting out that loud *haaaah*. Repeat 5 more times, and on the fifth time you drop the buckets and swing them behind you, just stay down there.

3 Release the buckets and remain in a forward hang. Let your breath find its own pace and depth as you just hang and let go. Stay for a few breaths and then inhale deeply as you slowly straighten your legs and roll your body up to standing. Once you are standing, exhale, close your eyes, and notice what's happening now.

Squat with Breath

1 Bend your knees and come down to a squat position slightly up on your toes with your heels off the floor. Your hands can help you balance by touching the floor between your feet, and your elbows are positioned inside your knees.

2 Lift your head and take a deep inhale. Drop your head between your knees while at the same time straightening your legs and raising your buttocks. Exhale as you go with a loud *haaaah*. Inhale as you come back to the squat. Exhale with a *haaaah* as you straighten your legs, raise your buttocks, and drop your head. You can do this exercise quite vigorously, which will elevate your heart rate and warm your body. Do it as vigorously as you can without exhausting yourself. The loud *haaaah* sound on the exhale will help get you moving. Repeat the sequence 5 more times and then just hang forward on the last cycle. Breathe.

3 After you hang for a few seconds, roll up to standing with an inhale. Follow that with a long, slow exhale when you arrive there. Close your eyes, breathe, and notice. Feel your whole body and notice anything else that might be happening right now.

Warrior

1 Stand at the back end of your mat. Take a large step forward with your left leg and then shift your body weight forward as you bend your left knee. Your left thigh should become parallel to the floor, and the lower part of that leg should be straight up and down to support your weight. The right leg should stay as straight as possible with the heel coming slightly off the floor.

2 Sweep your arms straight up over your head to shoulder width apart. Let your upper body be straight and fix your gaze on a spot directly out in front of you. Engage your breath with deep inhalation and long, slow exhalation—falling out. Hold the posture for just a few breaths to begin with. When you first practice this posture, you may not feel you can support it for very long. This is okay. One full breath is enough if that is all you can do. It is better to do this exercise as described and hold it for less time than it is to modify it to hold it longer. Over time, you will find that you can hold it longer and more easily, and you will begin to get the benefits of it, as well.

3 To come out of Warrior, straighten your left leg and step it back to join the right leg while at the same time lowering your arms with a long, slow exhale. Pause and notice as you take another deep breath.

4 Repeat the posture, this time stepping forward with the right leg. Again hold for just a few deep breaths and then step back to come out of the posture. Take a few moments to breathe and reflect. Notice what is happening now. Reflect on any feelings, thoughts, sensations, or images that came to you during the posture or that are there for you now. Just notice them. Then breathe and let it be.

Each and every yoga posture has a unique "feel" or quality to it. By paying attention, you will pick up on that feel. Sometimes the feel that a lot of people can relate to is inherent in the name of the posture, like this one: Warrior. However, I recommend that you discover the feel of the posture for yourself rather than attributing it to the name or anyone else's experience of it. At first, you may not get a clear hit on any quality or feel, especially the first time you are doing a posture. In the beginning, you will be trying to figure out how to do it and also may feel awkward, as your body is unfamiliar with yoga positions. I suggest you accept that. If awkwardness is your experience in the early stages, just let yourself be awkward, or whatever it is that you notice, for now. Later, as you are more familiar with the poses and are taking your time to slowly engage in them and feel them fully, your experience will change. And later, it may change again, and one quality may give way to another. This has happened to me many times over in 30 years of practice. Now each morning, even though I do much the same routine every day, I don't really know what to expect from one day to the next, and I don't try to anticipate anything. My morning yoga is like a journey of self-discovery, with new and different things to be observed in my body experience and about myself every day.

Chair

Chair Variation

✿

Repeat the posture, but this time begin from a position with your heels raised from the floor (on tiptoe). Raise your arms to the same position in front of you and come down to sit in the imaginary chair, but this time imagine that it is a straight-back chair and your back is against the back of it. (In other words, your back is straight, too.)

Hold the posture for 5 complete breaths and return to standing with an inhale. Lower your arms and your heels with an exhale. Breathe and notice.

1 Stand with your feet parallel, hip-width apart, and firmly planted on the floor. Bring your arms up to shoulder height straight out in front of you with palms facing down. Let go of any tension around your neck and shoulders with just a light effort to keep your arms up.

2 Slowly bend your legs at the knees and imagine you are resting the edge of your buttocks on the edge of an imaginary chair that is behind you. Hold that position and breathe for 5 full breaths before slowly returning to standing with a long inhale. When you are standing, exhale and lower your arms. Breathe and notice. What is happening now?

Transition to Floor

You are now at the midpoint of your practice, having completed the standing poses. Take another moment to reflect on this half of your practice. What have you noticed? What has been the most dominant aspect of your experience so far? Again, just notice and let it be for now.

Full Facedown Boat

1 After the Half Facedown Boat (see description on page 61), return to the floor and lengthen your arms and legs. Bring your focus to your center, or core. Lengthen your front and back from here, and press this mid-point of your body gently downward.

2 As you do this, you will notice a tendency for the arms and legs to want to lift as they lengthen. Let this happen and help it along a little, lifting both arms and both legs a few inches off the floor as you continue to lengthen them. Breathe deep breaths and also imagine this breath coming from and going to your core.

This posture may be difficult to sustain at the beginning. Just find a place you can come to where it works for you. It may be only 1 inch off the floor for only 1 or 2 breaths when you first start. Remember, it's not important how much you do or how far you go in each posture. What is more important is how you are with yourself and what you notice about yourself as you do it. And in order to generate that awareness, you have to be doing something with your body. A posture like this one can sometimes be quite intense as it moves things around. By engaging your body in this way, you change things from the inside. If you are able

to sustain the posture at your edge for even just a few breaths, you shift your way of being with yourself quite dramatically for a short time. This, in turn, allows awareness that may have been blocked to come to the surface.

A crude analogy might be to compare it with the use of a plunger on a sluggish drain. After a few strokes of the plunger, everything flows freely again. Sluggishness in our bodies can create sluggishness in our awareness. In turn, sluggish awareness can lead to choices that will create more stress. Finely tuned awareness can lead you to choices that lead to more bliss.

Bow

Benefits of Being Present

❋

I once had the privilege of leading a yoga workshop for a group of very obese people who were participating in a special diet program connected with Duke University. Some of them had cardiac problems or other illnesses, and some were in wheelchairs. When we presented to them the idea of doing a yoga workshop, many wanted to decline. I let them know that anybody can do yoga and assured them that they would just do what they could and that would be all that needed to happen. Most agreed to participate on that basis. I am not exaggerating when I tell you that several of them experienced life-changing awareness in the space of the few hours we worked together. They were able to do this by simply being fully present to their experience, whatever it happened to be. Had they allowed their preconceived ideas of what yoga was about to get in the way of their participating, or had they tried to do yoga by the book, this would not have occurred for them.

1 From a position facedown on your mat, come into the Full Boat posture.

2 Once in the posture, slowly sweep your arms around to the sides, bend your legs at the knees, and reach for your ankles with your hands. As you grasp your ankles, slowly extend your legs back to lift your chest farther from the floor. Lift your head and breathe deeply as you extend upward from the front and back, pressing your midsection into the floor. Take 3 full breaths and then slowly release the posture and return to a comfortable position facedown on the floor. Breathe and notice. What is happening now?

This is a somewhat advanced posture for many, and if you experience difficulty with it, simply replace it with the Full Facedown Boat as described. Go as far as you can with it, but stop short of any straining or struggling.

Child

1 From a position lying facedown, slowly draw your knees up under your body, sit on your heels, and place your head on the floor in front of your knees, and your arms back alongside your outer thighs.

2 Let go fully and breathe deeply. This is a great posture to hang out in and just be with yourself for a few minutes. Notice what happens as you do that. Observe, be aware, and accept.

Child Variations

✵

Child is a restorative posture. There should be no effort involved in being in it. If you have tight front thigh muscles, you may not be able to sit on your heels with ease. If this is the case, place a rolled-up blanket or a small pillow between your heels and your buttocks for support. If you have knee problems, this posture may aggravate them, and you can modify the posture so they don't hurt. For example, engage in a lying-down position.

Bridge

1 Lie on your back with your knees bent, feet flat on the floor up near your buttocks, and arms at your sides. Gently raise and lower the pelvis a few times to prepare for this posture. Breathe as you do. Then lift up your pelvis and hold it as high as you are able.

2 Without support, you probably won't be able to stay there for too long, so find a way to support the pelvis, chest, and torso in this elevated position. One option is to join your hands together under your body and use your arms as a lever. Alternately, you could place your hands under your buttocks or lower back, with your elbows on the floor, and let your arms

help support your body in its elevated position.

3 Once you have established the posture, you are going to bring your focus to different places on the front of your body for a few seconds each and for 1 or 2 full breaths. Begin by focusing on the area around your groin—the lowest part of your trunk. Breathe and notice what happens for you as you focus in this place. Just notice; no explanations needed. Then shift your awareness a few inches higher to a place just below your belly button. Breathe and focus here. What do you notice? Shift a little higher to the solar plexus at the base of the rib cage. Breathe and focus here. Again, what's

happening as you do this? Go to the next place: the center of your chest. Focus here, breathe, and notice. Then go to your throat. Breathe to and through your throat and notice as you do. Finally, bring your awareness to the whole front side of your upper body, from your groin to the crown of your head. Take a few more deep breaths as you focus and notice. Then with the next exhale, slowly let your body down and stretch out your legs along the floor. Stay present to what is happening as you take a few full breaths and let each exhale fall out. What is happening now? Notice.

Half-Seated Forward Bend

1 From a seated position, stretch your legs out in front of you. Keeping your right leg straight, bend your left leg at the knee and place your left foot next to the right side of your right knee.

2 Circle your left knee with your hands and/or arms and hug it in tight to your body. Straighten and lengthen your back. Breathe.

3 Inhale, and on the exhale, slowly move forward, with your chin leading the way, in the direction of your toes. Even though you are moving slightly forward, keep your back long and straight. Don't rush. Take at least 3 deep exhaling breaths to find your edge—not too much and not too little.

4 Once at the edge, take 3 more deep breaths and be fully present to the edge and all that happens there. What do you notice: feelings, thoughts, images, anything? What is happening now?

5 Slowly release the posture and continue to breathe and notice. Straighten out your legs, place your hands behind you, and lean back for a few seconds, letting go and breathing deep and easy breaths.

6 Repeat, this time with the right leg bent and the left leg straight.

Full-Seated Forward Bend

1 Begin in a seated position with your legs stretched out in front of you. Inhale and raise your arms out to the sides and up above your head. Lengthen and straighten your back. Imagine that there is an axle that goes from one hip to the other.

2 Slowly move forward from this axle, bending only a little on each full exhale. Find your edge by the third exhale and lower your arms in front of you to grasp your ankles or feet. Breathe and focus on the edge. Notice all that is happening: feelings, sensations, thoughts, images, anything. Hold for 3 more deep breaths and then slowly release back to a sitting position. Place your hands behind you with fingers pointing away and lean back for a few breaths. Return to the seated position. Watch and notice.

Lying Twist

1 From a position lying on your back, keep your right leg straight and bend your left leg at the knee, placing your left foot next to the right side of your right knee. Extend your left arm along the floor away from your shoulder at a 45-degree angle above your head. Turn your head to the left to look out along this arm.

2 Slowly allow your left knee to come across your body toward the right. Reach down with your right hand and place it on top of the knee to help it go down a little farther, creating a twist through your body from the left hip to the left shoulder. Find your edge in the twist and breathe. Watch and notice. What is happening now?

3 After 3 more deep breaths, slowly release out of the posture back to a lying position. Continue to notice and breathe.

4 Repeat Lying Twist with the right leg bent across the body toward the left.

5 Following the twist to the left, come to a position lying flat on your back with arms by your sides, palms facing up, and breathe—easy deep breaths—as you let go.

Wake-Up/Warm-Up Exercise

Your walks during your One-Day Personal Retreat will take on a slightly different format. They will consist of two parts. The new part will be slow, meditative walking, which will happen for the first 5 minutes of each walk. You may choose to do it indoors, or you can do it outdoors. If you are at all self-conscious about how you will appear to others when doing it outdoors, then maybe you would be better off doing it indoors, as it does look a little strange to someone who doesn't know what you are doing. Walking becomes a meditation when you bring your full attention and presence to the actual act of walking—that is, you do nothing else but walk.

Select a place where you can walk back and forth for 10 to 20 paces. Stand on one end. Feel your feet on the floor or ground. Be aware of yourself standing, and then begin to walk. Focus your attention on your body, feeling each step as you lift your foot and carefully place it back on the ground. Be relaxed about it, but walk with your body upright and spine long. Take enough time to be fully present and focused on each step you take. It may become a very slow walk as you do this. When you get to the end of your selected walking track, pause a moment, breathe 3 deep breaths, turn around, and repeat for another 10 to 20 steps.

Continue for a minimum of 5 minutes. You may find that by the second time you do this walk you can extend the time to 10 minutes. When you walk normally in life, you probably don't really focus on the act of walking itself. You are likely very busy in your mind, thinking about all kinds of things and becoming easily distracted by anything and everything going on around you. Here you are being asked to do the opposite. Simply be present to the act of walking one step at a time. Of course, you will be distracted by thoughts from time to time and by things around you. When this happens, just notice that it has happened, perhaps even labeling it by saying to yourself, "Aah…noticing distraction, aah… noticing thinking, noise, car, or whatever." Then return your focus to walking.

With some practice, you will be able to use walking as more than exercise. It will be a way of being present to yourself and what you are doing in the moment—walking.

When you go outside for your longer, more vigorous walk for the remaining 20 to 25 minutes, try to maintain the same meditative approach. Return after a total time of 30 minutes has elasped.

Meditation

During your One-Day Personal Retreat, there are two half-hour periods of meditation scheduled. This is longer than was previously suggested for this activity so far in this program, but by now you have been practicing long enough to be able to do this. As usual, make sure you are comfortable. Try to select a position you can maintain for the half hour, but if you have to change part of the way through, that is fine. Sitting is a preferred position if you can find one that works for you. You can meditate lying down, but it's easy to fall asleep, and as good as sleep is, and as much as you may need it, it's not meditation.

As you meditate, you can begin to watch your mind with a little more discernment. Try labeling and describing your thoughts and distractions as you notice them. For example, if you find yourself thinking about some future event that you anticipate will bring you great pleasure, you might say to yourself something like, "Noticing thinking—future, pleasant thought." Or if you notice yourself thinking about something you are afraid of, you could say to yourself, "Noticing fear." After each instance, simply take a breath and come back to just sitting, breathing, watching, noticing, accepting.

Final Exercise: Integration and Journaling

This exercise at the end of your One-Day Personal Retreat is designed to allow you to take what you have learned during this day and move forward. Most people who have followed this program report that this retreat was the most significant turning point for them. It is often this day that really determines a new direction with no turning back. The following exercise is one that I designed many years ago and have used in hundreds of workshops and training programs that I have led since. I call it the Heart-to-Heart Exercise. Here is how it goes.

Find a comfortable seated position. Close your eyes and breathe. Bring your left hand up to the middle of your chest and place it there. Breathe to the touch of your hand. Notice your hand on your chest, and for a few breaths, just be with the sensations and feelings that go with it. Then say the following to yourself: "Today I have seen myself in new ways. The awareness that has come to me today shows me that in my life I am imperfect in many ways. At a deeper level, however, I trust that I am like all other human beings, and that means being perfect in my imperfection. I am here in this life to learn and grow, and part of that learning is to see myself in my human form as being perfectly imperfect. By recognizing and accepting my imperfections, I have the opportunity to change if I choose to. I value that and am grateful for all awareness that gives me that opportunity. Beyond my human condition, I also trust that I am not alone. There is a deeper part to my existence that is linked to everything. There is a knowing that I have within me, a wisdom that can guide me. This wisdom that dwells within all beings is perfect and just right for me. I am growing to trust it more, and by listening to it more, I am learning to walk the path in life that is right for me."

Now raise your right hand as if you are reaching out to place it on the chest of someone sitting in front of you. You can, if you wish, imagine this to be someone you know, or let it be no one in particular. This person represents all others in your life, and your statement to the individual is as follows: "As I recognize my own perfection in my imperfection, I acknowledge it also in you and all beings. I offer you the space to grow and learn, as I am, and to change if you choose to, just as I am choosing what to change and what not to change. As I acknowledge the wisdom that is within me, I acknowledge it also within you and all beings, regardless of whether they see it or what they do with it. I honor the wisdom that dwells within me and all beings."

Now spend a few minutes going back over what you have noticed during the last day. What is significant? What tendencies in yourself did you notice? How do they appear in your life and contribute to your life? Do you see ways that you create stress? Do you see ways that you create happiness? Notice them all. Acknowledge them all. Accept them all. What about your relationship with yourself? How does it support or not support you in your life? Notice and accept it as it is for now, knowing that awareness is power.

Take a moment to close your eyes and go into silent meditation for a few minutes. Once you are there, seek out that place inside where you can find your wisdom, your knowing, your truth—the part of you that is your own best friend who loves you and knows the direction in life that is right for you. Ask for guidance. What do I do with all this awareness? What are one or two steps I could take that would make a difference? Listen and wait until the guidance comes to you. When you receive it, say it to yourself and visualize yourself acting on it as you say it. Make sure it fits your life. It doesn't help to just make it up or use one of my examples if it doesn't fit you.

I offer examples only to show how to do it, not what to do. The what must come from you. Let's say the guidance for someone was, "Have more fun in your life and create it." The person could say, "I am creating more fun in my life" while visualizing himself engaged in one of his favorite pastimes with a smile on his face and a great feeling throughout his body. It is important to link the words (phrased in first person, present tense, such as "I am…") with the action and with the body. Try saying it like that to begin with, and then try writing it that way in your journal. Remember that when you tap into your inner knowing when you meditate, you will only receive guidance that comes from a place of love for you, acceptance of you, and respect for you, regardless of whether you hold these feelings for yourself. If you don't get that guidance at first, just wait a little longer in silence until you do. If you can really wait and listen, you will be guided by the wisdom that is there for you.

You may think it would be a lot easier if I would have just written a book that told you what to do. It probably would, but it would not be as powerful or as effective in helping you. When the actions you take come directly from your own wisdom and apply directly to your life awareness, then not only will you realize the possibility of lasting change, but you will also begin a journey of trusting in yourself and acting from it that will serve you for the rest of your life. I think I said that earlier but want to say it again, as it's probably the single most important principle that this book is based upon.

Take the remainder of your half hour to write in your journal whatever you wish to say about your day, what you have learned, and what you plan to do with that knowledge. Finish by listing one or two simple actions that you can take right away and every day this week to make a difference. They don't have to be huge, earth-shattering acts, just simple steps to implement one day at a time.

Celebration

The last hour and a half of your day is reserved for celebration. If you have completed almost 24 hours in silence and followed all the exercises, you really do have something to celebrate. Not many people in this world have ever taken the time to do what you have just done. Also, you will no doubt have gained some valuable insights into your life. You may have found some things you want to change, but hopefully you will also have seen many of your strengths and that you have a life that is worthy of celebrating. This last hour and a half can be any kind of celebration that you choose, but it has to fit two basic rules. First, it has to be something that will be basically good for you and will not harm you in any way. Second, it must offer a way for you to genuinely celebrate yourself, and if it involves anyone else (which can be a great addition), the person or people you invite to celebrate with you must be on board for what you are wanting to celebrate and create in your life (no naysayers allowed).

Here are a few examples of how some people have chosen to celebrate. Remember, the celebration needs to genuinely reflect you—and how you want to put celebration into your life.

- Having a candlelight dinner with my partner to share what happened during the 24 hours
- Hiking to the top of a mountain with my dog and having a picnic
- Playing a round of golf with an old friend
- Taking a hot-air-balloon ride
- Getting a massage and a facial
- Going to my favorite restaurant
- Making a date with my girlfriends
- Shopping for that special something that I've been wanting
- Going to the zoo with my grandchildren
- Going fishing
- Buying that $30 bottle of wine to share at dinner
- Going for a swim at the beach
- Buying the CDs I've been wanting and dancing to them
- Spending time with an old friend I haven't seen in years

You can see from this list that there are a lot of different ways people have chosen to celebrate. Some of these probably resonate with you as celebratory things to do, and some likely don't. So forget the list above and write down the thing that really fits you. Then do it.

Sharing the Journey

This step is not included in the retreat but is something to be considered in the time following your day. If possible, find a friend or loved one with whom you can talk about the day. Find someone who can listen without offering advice. In fact, you can set it up that way by letting the person know you want to spend some time telling her about some important things that are happening for you in your life—that you are following a program that is helping you with these things and you want to share some of your experiences. Tell the person you don't need any advice; you just want her to hear you, and if she is to offer anything, let it be support by way of affirmation.

Alternatively, if you can't find someone who can fill that role, you might want to share your journey in a support group or with your therapist if you have one.

CHAPTER 6

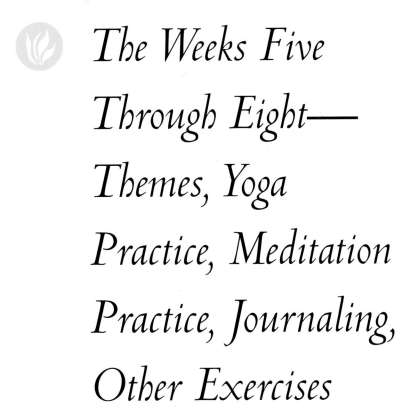

The Weeks Five Through Eight— Themes, Yoga Practice, Meditation Practice, Journaling, Other Exercises

CONGRATULATIONS! YOU ARE PAST THE HALFWAY MARK
with this program. The rest should be a lot easier because you
are now getting used to working with yourself in this way. On
the other hand, this is also the time to be vigilant with your
commitment. Remember, one day at a time, make the commitment each day for the following day, and also remember that
you are doing this to support your intention of what you want
to create in your life. Remember what that is? Might be a good
idea to say it to yourself again: "What I want to create in my
life by following this program is…"

For the next 4 weeks, your yoga and meditation practice will
basically follow the same format, alternating days spent
focused on yoga and meditation. And again, each week will
have a theme for your self-inquiry.

WEEK FIVE

The theme for this week is *discernment*. Exactly what does that mean? A simple nondictionary definition that I like is simply *noticing the difference*. When you're practicing becoming more aware and more mindful, it's a step up to be able to discern one kind of awareness from another. It's kind of like a child who has an early experience of eating ice cream. At first, the child notices she's eating ice cream but has no awareness of flavor. Later, she notices the difference between chocolate and strawberry flavors and is practicing discernment. An ice cream connoisseur will be able to discern between Ben and Jerry's vanilla and Hood brand vanilla.

This week, you can try practicing discernment with ice cream if you want, but better still, try to notice the subtle differences in your awareness of thoughts, feelings, sensations, desires, preferences, friends, choices, and so on. Those of us who like the experience of dining out at restaurants begin to make subtle comparisons between the food at one restaurant and the food at another. But do we learn to notice the subtle differences about many other things in our lives? For example, do we look at a sunset and just see another sunset? Or do we distinguish between the subtleties of the colors, the air, the humidity, the overall feel of it, the feelings we have at the moment we're looking at it, and so on? If you think about it, no two sunsets are the same, and certainly no two experiences we have of them are the same. Can we notice the differences? The same applies to our experiences of ourselves moment to moment. There are subtle differences in everything about us and everything in which we are engaging.

Week Five

Set aside 40-45 minutes each day to practice.

SUNDAY

Noticing and Discerning—Focus and Intention

Setting: **2 minutes**

Yoga Practice Sequence: **28 minutes**

Meditation and Integration: **5 minutes**

Journaling: **5 minutes**

* *Take at least five 20-second awareness breaks today*
* *Practice accepting all that you notice*
* *Notice also what you are currently choosing*
* *Notice the subtle differences in everything: Learn to discern*
* *Drink 8 glasses of water today*
* *Act on a choice today that will support your intention*
* *Schedule a treat for your body for later this week*

MONDAY

Noticing and Discerning—Focus and Intention

Setting: **2 minutes**

Sitting Meditation Exercise: **15 minutes**

Walking: **15 minutes**

Integration: **3 minutes**

Journaling: **5 minutes**

* *Take at least five 20-second awareness breaks today*
* *Practice accepting all that you notice*
* *Notice also what you are currently choosing*
* *Notice the subtle differences in everything: Learn to discern*
* *Drink 8 glasses of water today*
* *Act on a choice today that will support your intention*

TUESDAY

Noticing and Discerning—Focus and Intention

Setting: **2 minutes**

Yoga Practice Sequence: **28 minutes**

Meditation and Integration: **5 minutes**

Journaling: **5 minutes**

* *Take at least five 20-second awareness breaks today*
* *Practice accepting all that you notice*
* *Notice also what you are currently choosing*
* *Notice the subtle differences in everything: Learn to discern*
* *Drink 8 glasses of water today*
* *Act on a choice today that will support your intention*

WEDNESDAY

Noticing and Discerning—Focus and Intention

Setting: **2 minutes**

Sitting Meditation Exercise: **15 minutes**

Freezer Exercise: **15 minutes**

Integration: **3 minutes**

Journaling: **5 minutes**

* *Take at least five 20-second awareness breaks today*
* *Practice accepting all that you notice*
* *Notice also what you are currently choosing*
* *Notice the subtle differences in everything: Learn to discern*
* *Drink 8 glasses of water today*
* *Act on a choice today that will support your intention*

Th

THURSDAY

Noticing and Discerning—Focus and Intention Setting: **2 minutes**

Yoga Practice Sequence: **28 minutes**

Meditation and Integration: **5 minutes**

Journaling: **5 minutes**

* Take at least five 20-second awareness breaks today
* Practice accepting all that you notice
* Notice also what you are currently choosing
* Notice the subtle differences in everything: Learn to discern
* Drink 8 glasses of water today
* Act on a choice today that will support your intention

F

FRIDAY

Noticing and Discerning—Focus and Intention Setting: **2 minutes**

Sitting Meditation Exercise: **15 minutes**

Walking: **15 minutes**

Integration: **3 minutes**

Journaling: **5 minutes**

* Take at least five 20-second awareness breaks today
* Practice accepting all that you notice
* Notice also what you are currently choosing
* Notice the subtle differences in everything: Learn to discern
* Drink 8 glasses of water today
* Act on a choice today that will support your intention

Sa

SATURDAY

(If you have already completed 6 days this week, then this day is optional. If you don't want to practice, spend an hour doing something you really love to do.)

Noticing and Discerning—Focus and Intention Setting: **2 minutes**

Yoga Practice Sequence: **28 minutes**

Meditation and Integration: **5 minutes**

Journaling: **5 minutes**

* Take at least five 20-second awareness breaks today
* Practice accepting all that you notice
* Notice also what you are currently choosing
* Notice the subtle differences in everything: Learn to discern
* Drink 8 glasses of water today
* Act on a choice today that will support your intention

Noticing and Discerning—Focus and Intention Setting

This week begins in the usual way of breathing, noticing, and accepting what is happening in your body, your breath, and your feelings and thoughts. Then begin to discern the difference between some feelings and others, some thoughts and others. Play with your breath a little. Notice how different ways of breathing feel. Then ask yourself, "What is it that I really want to create in my life?" As you reflect on the question, try to discern more carefully between what you want and what you do not want.

Yoga Practice Sequence

This week on Sunday and Thursday, you will refer to the "Longer Yoga Sequence" on page 118, and after completing the focus and intention exercise, you will do all the even-numbered postures. On Tuesday and Saturday after the focus and intention exercise, you will do all the odd-numbered postures, as well as the last one: Corpse (number 26). If you have any extra time available and want to do the complete longer routine on any of the days, then this would be a great thing to do at this stage of your program. However, doing extra on one day does not work as a substitute for missing a day. Make sure to do at least 40 minutes every day—one day at a time.

As you practice your yoga this week, try to discern between different feelings and sensations that you experience from moment to moment in each posture. Look for the subtle differences in the quality of your experience.

Meditation

In your sitting meditation this week, also focus on the theme of discernment. Notice the different thoughts and different kinds of thoughts. See if you can label your experience as you meditate—for example, "Noticing thinking—sad thoughts," "Noticing feeling—calm feelings," "Noticing body—restless sensations," and so on.

Walking

As you walk this week, look around you for things you have never noticed before on your walks. Also practice looking inward, as you do in your meditation practice, and label your moment-to-moment experiences as you walk.

Freezer Exercise

Instead of your walk on Wednesday, take 15 minutes of your practice time to look in your freezer. Notice what different things are in there and label them in your mind— for example, "Peas—have for dinner tomorrow," "Frozen fruit-juice cubes—here since last summer," and so on. Do an inventory of all the items you can find. What subtle feelings and thoughts come up as you do this? What do you notice about yourself and your life from this exploration of your freezer? Just notice for now. There is no need to do anything unless you feel absolutely compelled to start throwing things out or rearranging them.

Integration

For the next 4 weeks, the daily integration exercise will be slightly different. Here is how it goes.

Reflect back on what you noticed during your practice. In particular, look for any awareness about yourself that came to you. Ask yourself, "How does this connect to or show up in my life?" Acknowledge and accept whatever answer comes from asking that question. Next, connect to your inner wisdom—the place within you that knows you, loves you, supports you, and wants to guide you in a loving and unselfish way—and seek guidance by asking, "What do I do with this awareness? What can I do differently in my life as a result? What change could I make that would really make a difference for me? And what would be the first step I would need to take to move in that direction?" Listen in silent meditation for a few moments until the answers to these questions come. Repeat the questions to yourself several times if you need to.

Journaling

For the next 4 weeks, write in your journal daily:

1. Note what guidance you receive from your integration.

2. Note any other observations you make about yourself as you go through life each day, particularly any changes you are noticing as a result of your increased awareness.

WEEK SIX

The theme for Week Six is *discovering personal truth*—in other words, what is really true for you as opposed to what you might have thought was true before. As you have progressed through this program, if you have been following the themes and doing the daily practices, you will have become more aware of yourself. You will know yourself a little better as a result. You may have been able to accept what you have learned about yourself. Further, you may have seen that you now have more choice in your life, and you have explored your relationship to yourself and have been able to discern subtle differences in your experience of life. If you have done all this, you are ready to decide what is, at this time, true for you.

Our truth changes as we go through life, and so I believe it is important from time to time to ask ourselves what is really true for us now as opposed to what might have been true before. Shortly before writing this book, I decided to take the time ask myself what was really true for me now at this time in my life. Here are just 10 items from my list to show you how one's truth can cover many different aspects of life.

1. I love my family very much and want to spend more time with each family member.

2. I want to spend more time writing and less time managing the affairs of my organization.

3. I tend to think a lot about the future and spend a lot of my thought time in future planning. This is fine, but I want to increase the amount of time I spend in the present. I want to take the time to watch a sunset every chance I get.

4. I love to travel but not quite as much as I used to.

5. Every time I go to Maine, particularly to my cabin in the North Woods, I appreciate the beauty there and feel very good inside myself.

6. The house in which I've been living in no longer suits my family's needs.

7. I have a few very good quality work relationships and want to contribute significantly to those relationships in the future.

8. The quality of my children's education is important to me.

9. I like to cook and enjoy good food and am no longer a vegetarian.

10. My spiritual practice is now less a formality and has become more a part of my life and how I try to live mindfully each moment of each day.

This week, I invite you to take the time to find the statements that describe your truth for now. It is important that you distinguish your truth from your desires (another opportunity to practice discernment). Your truth is a multitude of statements that describe what is true for you now in your life. Although your truth is not permanent, it is not superficial or transitory. It goes a little deeper than the temporary desire for food, sex, or sleep, for example.

In Weeks Six, Seven, and Eight, your basic yoga and meditation practice is the same as for Week Five. There are different themes for you to focus on each week, however, and you should build the focus of these themes into each aspect of your daily practice as follows.

Discovering Personal Truth—Focus and Intention Setting

This week at the beginning of each daily practice, as you breathe and focus on your breath and body, ask yourself, "What do I notice right now that is true for me?"

Yoga Practice Sequence

As you practice yoga this week (as programmed for Week Five), take the time to breathe between each posture and pose this question to yourself: "What is true for me right now?" Silently answer the question before moving on to the next posture.

Meditation

As you meditate this week and watch your thoughts and your feelings, notice your desires and label each one as "desire." Notice also any indications of your truth and label them as "truth" or "maybe truth" if you are not certain.

Walking

As you walk this week, imagine that you are looking out ahead of you in your life. Where are you headed? What are you walking toward? What are you leaving behind?

Self-Observation Exercise

On Wednesday this week instead of walking, take 15 minutes to make the following two lists:

1. Write down everything you can remember picking up to read in the last week, including any magazines or journals you subscribe to and read as soon as you can after they arrive. (Also notice any you may subscribe to and don't read, but don't put them on your list.)

2. Write down all the places in which you have spent time during the last week and felt some degree of contentment or happiness.

Read over your lists. What do they tell you about what might be true for you?

Integration

Follow the instructions in Week Five.

Journaling

Follow the instructions in Week Five and add any items to your list of personal truths.

WEEK SEVEN

Your theme for this week is *truth in action*—noticing what you might be able to do to put your truth into action. It should be in the form of simple steps.

As you develop your list of truths, look over them and ask, "What might I be able to do this week that would be one small step toward putting these into action?" As you begin this process, use your daily practice as a time to sit with both the intention you may be setting for yourself and any awareness you may get as you begin to act on your truths. You may notice joy, exhilaration, fear, worry, hesitation, discomfort, happiness, contentment, or any multitude of feelings and thoughts. Try to notice them all and simply be present to them as you do. Let your yoga and meditation this week be a time-out from putting your truth into action in your daily life—a time-out to just be present to yourself and let it be. Toward the end of this week, take time during your integration to look over your list of truths and reflect on actions you may have taken or may be contemplating. Notice what has happened. Ask for guidance around any difficulties you may be having and write any guidance you receive in your journal.

Here are a few examples of truth in action, along with things noticed, taken from my list of truths.

1. Truth: I want more time with my family. Action: Schedule dinner once per week with adult children and their families. Noticed: Some resistance on my part to doing this, using excuses of "being too busy" and "needing to plan too far ahead."
Guidance: Stay the distance. Don't make excuses. Take the time to make it happen if you really want it.

2. Truth: House no longer suits family. Action: Talk with family about concerns and what they might want. Noticed: My wanting to make the decision myself. Guidance: If you involve them, it's a way of loving them. Take the time.

I offer these two examples because they were instrumental in providing me with yet another important awareness: My impatience sometimes stops me from taking the time to create what I really want in my life!

Truth in Action—Focus and Intention Setting

At the beginning of each practice session this week, notice your intention in relation to acting on your truth. What does acting on truth involve and what do you intend?

Yoga Practice Sequence

Let each posture (as programmed for Week Five) become an opportunity to act on your moment-to-moment truth. What does your body want right now? Ask, "How can I adjust this posture to reflect my truth and act on it?"

Meditation

What thoughts do you notice that lead you to act on your truth? What thoughts do you notice that get in the way of that?

Walking

As you walk this week, notice what it is you want to walk toward in your life. Visualize it and feel it in your body as you walk. What can you do to act more fully on walking your truth into your life?

Acting-on-Truth Exercise

In place of a walk on Wednesday, take 15 minutes of your practice time to reflect on these two questions and make two lists. Question 1: In what ways am I putting my truth into action in my life? Question 2: What gets in my way of doing more of this?

Integration

Notice all that you have discovered about your truth and your desire to act upon it. Seek guidance around what other steps you might be able to take to put your awareness into action.

Journaling

Write a few notes to yourself about how able or unable you are to act on your truth and to put your new awareness about yourself into action in your life.

WEEK EIGHT

The theme for this week is *flow*. Once you have found out how to use the practices outlined in this book and you are able to practice regularly, you will find that there will be a flow to your life. It works a little like the example above. As a result of taking action on my truths discovered from these practices, I received yet another awareness about myself. That may seem disheartening to some: "Here I am doing all these practices, and I'm not done! There is more!" Sure there is. But notice the increase in clarity associated with that awareness. And notice the power it offers. I can choose to let my impatience be a barrier, or I can notice it and work around it. Until I was aware of it, however, I was powerless to change it. My impatience would just get in the way time and time again without my even knowing it.

Part of flow is the continual re-creation of yourself as you get to know yourself better. A daily practice like what you have been doing for the past 7 weeks is one of the best ways to get into a flow in your life. Flow is a little like the phoenix rising. Like the mythical phoenix, if you are in a flow, you are constantly dying to who you were and being born to who you are becoming. You are letting go of the old you and welcoming the new you on a regular and ongoing basis. So this week as you practice, begin to learn to recognize the flow in your daily life as you become more aware of it, more accepting of it, and more willing to act on it.

Your program is basically the same as for Week Seven with the addition of taking time to notice the flow in your life that you have created as a result of your increased awareness and willingness to act on your truth.

Flow—Focus and Intention Setting

At the beginning of each practice session this week, notice your intention in relation to creating flow in your life. What does the creation of flow involve and what do you intend?

Yoga Practice Sequence

Let your practice this week (as programmed for Week Five) flow from one posture to the next. Notice the flow of sensations, feelings, thoughts, and images as you practice. Just notice the flow. Notice also any interruption of the flow and what creates it. Accept that.

Meditation

Distinguish between *flowing thoughts,* which support the flow in your life, and *blocking thoughts,* which don't support your flow. Do the same with feelings that come up and your responses to those feelings.

Walking

As you walk this week, notice the flow or lack of it in your step. Connect it to your life. How would you be in your body to create more flow? How would you be in your life to create more flow?

Notes-to-Myself Exercise

On Wednesday this week instead of walking, take 15 minutes of your practice time to write two notes to yourself. The first note is to your old self to say good-bye to those aspects of yourself you no longer need to take with you on your journey. Your second note is to your new self to welcome those aspects of yourself that you are discovering that you want to take with you. In this note, also list everything that you feel you have accomplished in your life as a result of following this program over the past 8 weeks.

Integration

Notice all that you have discovered so far in this program and how it connects to your life. Notice what you are choosing to do with what you've discovered. Seek guidance around what other steps you might be able to take to put your awareness into action.

Journaling

Write down steps you are taking and will be taking. Write down all you have accomplished so far and where you see yourself headed now. Add to your list of truths as you become aware of them. Write down any commitments you want to make to yourself for the future.

CHAPTER 7

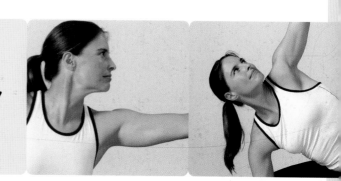

Reflections and Moving on

SO YOUR 8 WEEKS HAVE PASSED AND YOU WILL BE ABLE TO look back and see what has happened. If you have followed the program perfectly for the 8 weeks, that's great, and you will undoubtedly be noticing some benefit. If you have followed most of the program most of the time, you should also be noticing some benefit. If you have struggled to stay with the program and have done only bits and pieces, hopefully that will have been enough for you to know that it has possibilities for you, and you may want to make a clean start and try it again from the beginning. This is the kind of program you can repeat many times over, and each time you do it, it will be different. You will notice things the second time that you missed the first, and the benefits will be cumulative. I've had clients repeat the program three times within a year and then continue with a daily practice based on the program beyond that. They say it becomes an integral part of their lives after a while and offers them tremendous ongoing benefits.

As you look back and notice how much or little of the program you were able to stay with, also look back at the highlights for you. What stood out as an important turning point and how has that affected your life? Are you any clearer now as to how you end up creating stress in your life and how you can turn your stress into bliss? Take the Simple Bliss Test in Appendix One again and look at your score. Is it higher than it was at the beginning?

Assuming you have been able to make a difference in your life over the past 8 weeks, where do you go now? What do you want to build into your life from here on that will continue to support you in creating what you want? If you want to create more bliss and less stress in your life into the future, you need to set up your life in ways that will support that. What do you think has been the best support for you during this program? Which aspects of this program made the most difference for you, and how would you go about building more of that into your life? If you have followed the program, you will have noticed that it isn't just the practices themselves that make the difference. It's the way you practice, and the awareness you get as a result, that begins to make the difference. Then it's what you choose to do with that awareness in an ongoing way that really leads to benefits. It's not easy to live your life mindfully. It's much easier to just react to situations as they come up. It's easier to be a victim of circumstance than it is to choose the path that will make a difference. That is an option we face every day in almost every moment. What I have personally discovered, however, is that once I have begun to see that I have choice and spend less time being a victim of circumstance, it becomes more and more attractive to live that way. The daily practices also allow me sufficient breathing space in my day to remind myself of what I want and what I need to do to help create it. So taking that little amount of time each day (preferably, a minimum of 40 minutes) is a great way to keep the ball rolling in the direction we want.

Other things that will help include friendships or partnerships where there is a mutual commitment to growth and living mindfully. This does not mean doing everything the same. In fact, it's more about respecting difference. We all express our lives differently, so it is important to have friendships and partnerships that support that while allowing an ongoing commitment to our own growth and that of others at a very deep level. We're not all lucky enough to have this, but it is something we can work toward if we so choose. If it's not present in our primary relationships, we can perhaps find it with friends or within a support group, a yoga community, a church, or some other organization. Be wary of friends who constantly offer you advice (often unsolicited). They may be fun people with whom to engage in a variety of activities, but advice givers are not the best people to support you in changing your life for the better. As you did in this program, you need to feel comfortable trusting your own choices, acting from your own wisdom, and dancing to the beat of your own drum. Friends who also know how to do this and support your doing it by simply listening to you with interest and without offering suggestions are the best kind of friends to surround yourself with.

In the same vein, be wary of teachers who want to give you the answers for life. You will find an abundance of such teachers everywhere in every facet of life. Many yoga teachers are like this. They gain some knowledge and then want to convert everyone to their way of thinking and their prescription for life. Again, this is not what you need if you want to live mindfully and empower yourself to find your own unique path. What kind of teacher should you look for? Here is a list of criteria that I have kept ever since I first read it some 3 decades ago. It comes from the book *The Aquarian Conspiracy,* by Marilyn Ferguson. She sees the kind of teacher that best supports growth as one who…

- is also learning and is transformed by the relationship with his or her students;

- respects the learners' autonomy;

- knows that learning can't be imposed and helps the individual discover it within;

- is a steersman, a catalyst, a facilitator—an agent of learning but not the first cause;

- has a healthy level of self-esteem, little defensiveness, and few ego needs;

- sees learning as a process rather than a product;

- liberates the self, opens the eyes, makes the learner aware of choice. (We only learn what we always knew.)

If you are seeking a teacher who will support you in your inner life journey, look for one with these qualities.

Whether you choose a teacher or choose to be your own steersman, you will from time to time encounter resistance to change. It's often much easier not to change even when we know without doubt that changes need to be made. As this happens for just about everyone choosing to live more mindfully, I will offer a few suggestions as to how to respond when you notice your resistance kicking in.

First, you need to clarify what is really happening for you. For example, you

notice yourself thinking, "I know if I am to do my yoga and meditation practice this morning before I go to work, I need to get of bed now. I don't want to get out of bed. I just want to lie here for another 20 minutes. And I'm kind of tired of all this practice stuff and not too sure it's even helping me."

After noticing this line of thinking, you need to clarify what is happening: "I am lying in bed, noticing that I want to stay here and noticing how I'm finding arguments to support not doing my practice today. I'm noticing my resistance to it."

The next step is to remember what inspired you at the beginning. Ask, "Why did I choose to do this program in the first place?" Listen for your answer. Then ask, "Do I still want that?" Listen for a yes or a no. If the answer is yes, then ask, "What choice could I make in this moment that will best support me in getting that? What is the risk if I do that? What is the potential reward if I do that?" Weigh the risk and the reward and make a choice.

If the answer is no, then you are at the end of the road on this particular path and need to once again search inside for what it is you want in your life and what choices will best support that. Regardless, you will come to a choice point that causes you either to yield to your resistance or to choose something else. You will be aware of what you want to create in your life and what potential risks and rewards are associated with taking or not taking a particular action. And whatever you choose, accept it. After all, no one is saying you have to go this way or that way. It's not that one way is good and another way is bad. It's a pragmatic issue. You either choose to do what supports you in getting what you want in your life, or you don't. It's really that simple.

Some people believe that courage means facing ordeals without fear or resistance, maybe like the warrior going into battle. In truth, however, the real hero, the real warrior, is not the one without fear and resistance but the one who has fear and resistance, acknowledges it, and goes ahead anyway. If we are to change our lives and live more fully and with greater freedom and power, we will meet both resistance and fear somewhere along the road. Such resistance and fear can be used as a source of re-commitment or as a barrier to further growth. One of the key ideas behind this program is to use your stress to create your bliss. This means first getting in touch with yourself to the extent that you know what you do to create the life you are currently creating. Knowing what you do when you encounter resistance to following a chosen path is something that can be useful to you if you are willing to notice it, accept it, and decide what you want to do about it from here on. So make friends with the part of you that resists this program. Get to know it and decide what to do with it each time you meet it.

One last thing that I want to address in this book is the issue of change that I briefly mentioned in the beginning. I believe that increasing our capacity to effectively manage change in our lives is one of the most significant things we can do to produce a more blissful and less stressful life. There are two main areas of change that we face. One is change that occurs on the outside: things, events, and circumstances happening in the world around us. Clearly, what happened in America on September 11, 2001, is a prime example. Other examples may be more personal and less catastrophic, such as moving one's residence from one city to another. The other type of change occurs inside of us: growing older, changing health, changing needs and wants, growing more aware, seeing things differently than before, and so on. Inside changes are more subtle and often more difficult to recognize than the changes occurring in our world around us, but they can also be sources of stress if not effectively managed.

The first and most significant way of effectively managing change is to become aware that the change has happened and to realize what impact the change has upon us and our lives. In the months and years following 9/11, the area in western Massachusetts where I lived underwent a huge upsurge in real estate sales to people leaving the city for a more sedate rural lifestyle. In talking to many of these folks, I learned that it wasn't necessarily or exclusively the terrorist attack that had made them move. It was something they had been considering for a long time, but the events of that day in September were the final catalyst they needed to prompt them to action. The awareness of what they had wanted to create in their lives had been there for some time but had not been sufficiently clear to move them to action. It took a catalyst to do that. The people I talked to also mentioned that they had been under stress for many years and were relieved to have finally done something different to change that.

My question is, How can we put ourselves ahead of the game? How can we get the clarity we need and the resolve to act on our awareness before a catastrophic event moves us? I believe it is the processes and exercises that I have described in this book that can help. These processes involve the use of both our bodies and our minds. They help us do things in a way that brings us home to ourselves and encourages us to trust ourselves more—to notice and accept what we are currently doing and move to a new way of being by taking the actions we need to support it. I know that following this kind of path is not always easy in the beginning. It's a very different approach to life than what many of us know or have been taught to follow. It's also an ongoing journey to deeper levels of knowledge and awareness rather than to a final destination. It's a journey that requires courage, commitment, self-generated power, and above all, the recognition within ourselves that we are unique and wonderful human beings.

APPENDIX ONE

 Additional Resources

All of the following materials are available from Phoenix Rising Yoga Therapy Center: www.pryt.com or 800-288-9642.

PROGRAM AUDIO CDS

Yoga: It's about Life, a set of eight short yoga experiences led by author Michael Lee that matches the themes of this 8-week program

Phoenix Rising Therapeutic Yoga, a longer 80-minute experience led by Michael Lee that includes all 26 postures listed for this program

Yoga with Your Mate, a 1-hour Phoenix Rising Partner Yoga experience led by Michael Lee

BOOKS AND ARTICLES

Phoenix Rising Yoga Therapy: A Bridge from Body to Soul, by Michael Lee (Health Communications, 1997)

Articles written by Michael Lee available for free downloading at www.pryt.com

PROFESSIONAL RESOURCES

Information on becoming a Phoenix Rising Yoga Therapy practitioner or a Phoenix Rising Yoga teacher

An international listing of certified Phoenix Rising Yoga Therapy practitioners and advanced practitioners and certified Phoenix Rising Yoga teachers

SHARE YOUR STORY WITH THE AUTHOR

If you would like to tell the author and others about your experience with the program presented in this book, go to www.turnstressintobliss.com. You can sign up for a free newsletter about managing stress in your life. Feel free to email the author at author@turnstressintobliss.com.

APPENDIX
TWO

Simple Bliss Test

Take this test before you begin your 8-week program and again after you complete it. This test is not meant to be used as a scientific instrument, but it will give you an overall idea of the extent of the stress and bliss in your life. Compare your score at the end of the 8 weeks with your score from the beginning, and it will indicate what you have achieved by following this program.

Rate each item on a scale of 0 to 10 in terms of how accurately it describes you. A 0 would be "Does not describe me at all," a 5 would be "Sometimes describes me," and a 10 would be "Always describes me."

1. I am a happy person.

2. I have a clear purpose in my life that I'm pleased about.

3. I am achieving what I want in my life.

4. The stress in my life is moderate and manageable.

5. I am patient and calm in times of struggle.

6. I take good care of my physical and emotional health.

7. My life is exciting and challenging.

8. I get pleasure regularly from helping others.

9. There are people in my life who love me and who I enjoy spending time with.

10. My work is meaningful to me and serves others.

Total score out of a possible 100 _____

Results: If you scored 0 to 30, you don't have a lot of bliss in your life, and you're probably experiencing one or more symptoms of stress. If you scored 31 to 60, you could probably use more bliss in your life, but you may not notice you feel all that stressed-out. If you scored 61 to 100, maybe you should be writing this book!

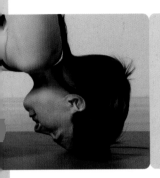

Phoenix Rising
Therapeutic Yoga

COMPLETE POSTURE LIST

1. Focus and Intention Setting
2. Wake-up/Warm-Up Exercise
3. Cat and Dog
4. Standing Body Scan
5. Falling-Out Breath/Stillness
6. Neck and Shoulder Stretch
7. Three-Part Breath
8. Swinging Twist
9. Heavy Bucket Swing
10. Squat with Breath
11. Side Bend (Half-Moon)
12. Back Bend
13. Standing Forward Bend
14. Warrior
15. Chair
16. Half and Full Facedown Boat
17. Bow
18. Cobra
19. Child
20. Knees to Chest
21. Bridge
22. Half-Seated Forward Bend
23. Full-Seated Forward Bend
24. Knees to Chest
25. Lying Twist
26. Corpse

ACKNOWLEDGMENTS

I wish to thank my wife, Lori, her entire family, and my children and their families, for their constant support and for taking care of business at home while I went to Maine to write. Special thanks to my children, Josh, Shannon, Jack and his friend Luca, for joining me in Maine and contributing their loving presence to my writing environment, and for staying asleep in the early mornings while I wrote. I honor the legacy of the spirit left by my mother and father, who always believed in me and encouraged me to do what I love.

I thank my longtime colleague, Karen Hasskarl, our dedicated staff, and all the Phoenix Rising practitioners and trainees for their support and commitment to taking this work into the world. I thank all of my teachers helped me learn and grow over the years.

Thanks to photographer Allan Penn and model Dianne Parisi, for the professional photo shoot and for including my son, Jack, in the fun. A very big thanks to Donna Raskin, my editor, for her clarity and vision, for inviting me to write this book, and supporting me along the way.